ONE WEEK

LEISURE, LIFESTYLE AND THE NEW MIDDLE CLASS

Who are the new middle class and how do they live?

Conducted within the theoretical context associated with the work of Pierre Bourdieu, Derek Wynne looks at how the new middle class goes about constructing and defending its social identity.

Through the study of residents living on a recently constructed housing estate, 'The Heath', which contains its own private leisure and sports facilities, he considers the extent to which social identity within the new middle class can be considered to relate more to experiences associated with leisure and cultural consumption than to experiences related to productive activity.

Derek Wynne is Senior Lecturer in the Department of Sociology, Manchester Metropolitan University.

LEISURE, LIFESTYLE AND THE NEW MIDDLE CLASS

A case study

Derek Wynne

London and New York

First published 1998
by Routledge
11 New Fetter Lane, London EC4P 4EE

Simultaneously published in the USA and Canada
by Routledge
29 West 35th Street, New York, NY 10001

Reprinted 1999, 2000 (twice), 2001

Routledge is an imprint of the Taylor & Francis Group

Typeset in Palatino by RefineCatch Limited, Bungay, Suffolk
Printed and bound in Great Britain by
T.J.I. Digital, Padstow, Cornwall

British Library Cataloguing in Publication Data
A catalogue record for this book is available from the British Library

Library of Congress Cataloguing in Publication Data
Wynne, Derek.
Leisure, lifestyle, and the new middle class: a case study/
Derek Wynne.
p.   cm.
Includes bibliographical references and index.
1. Middle class—Recreation—England—Sociological aspects—Case
studies. 2. Leisure—England—Sociological aspects—Case studies.
3. Middle class—England—Social life and customs—Case studies.
I. Title.
GV14.45.W95   1998
306.4'812'0941—DC21   97–21482

ISBN 0–415–03834–0

To Jenny, Mat and Kirsti

CONTENTS

FIGURES

TABLES

PREFACE

This study examines the social construction of identity within the new middle class within a theoretical context associated with the work of Pierre Bourdieu. It considers the extent to which social identity within the new middle class can be considered to relate more to experiences associated with leisure and cultural consumption than to experiences related to productive activity, and the development of this position is used to examine the degree to which class itself can *still* be seen as the primary determinant of identity.

Using Bourdieu's theoretical schema the book considers (i) the extent to which the new middle class or service class can be considered an homogenous grouping; (ii) whether the formation of the new middle class can be primarily understood through a social mobility accounted for by an increasing 'credentialism' or (iii) whether other forms of social mobility associated with occupational change have resulted in a new middle class which is *essentially* fragmented.

Following a discussion of previous work the book reports the findings of a case study undertaken on a private housing estate located in the Cheshire 'green belt'. The findings are supportive of a cultural heterogeneity within the new middle class(es) which lends support to contemporary sociological theorising on both the formation of the new middle class and contemporary cultural change.

ACKNOWLEDGEMENTS

To the people on The Heath, thanks for your time, and I hope that you find this an acceptable reflection.

To Ken Roberts whose patience, support, good humour and insight are among the main reasons that this project was completed. Thanks Ken.

To Mike Featherstone, to whose writings, ideas, conversations and encouragement I am clearly indebted. Thanks Mike.

To John Urry, editor of this series, and Mari Shullaw at Routledge, thanks for your encouragement, and patience.

To the many friends and colleagues who gave their help and support in many different ways over the period that this project was undertaken. Those with whom I talked through ideas, pored over data or just rambled to include Dave Bennett, Pete Bramham, Eric Corijn, Phil Mole, Hans Mommaas, Justin O'Connor, Dianne Phillips, Gary Pollock, Steve Redhead, Julian Tanner and Jenny Wynne. Thank you all.

Finally, where would I have been without Jenny, Mat and Kirsti? Thanks for putting up with me.

1

INTRODUCTION

This study consists of an empirical analysis of residents living on a recently constructed housing estate which contains its own private leisure and sports facilities – The Heath. Without wishing to pre-empt a necessary discussion of these terms it can be characterised as a case study of the new middle class. It began as an attempt to monitor the use of the sports and leisure facilities that the residents of this large, private housing estate enjoy, and to discover whether the existence of such facilities produced greater levels of participation amongst them as compared to socio-economically similar populations whose access to sports facilities were less readily available. However, in documenting the use of these facilities it soon became apparent that there were other, much more interesting activities to document in relating the role that such facilities played on The Heath.

There is a long history in community studies, and sociological investigation generally, of 'things not being quite what they first seemed'. Personal accounts of, and reflections on, the research process are replete with stories of researchers finding themselves in situations which they had not planned for and reorienting their research activities (Wild, 1978; Bryson and Thompson, 1978). Indeed as Bell and Newby (1971) indicate in their review and discussion of the 'community study as method' such research *method* is best understood as a *process* during which the researcher(s) will inevitably be faced with decisions regarding the path to be followed next, the relative importance of one set of observations over another and the theoretical weight of the events that are recorded. Rather than seeing this as a problematic feature of the community study as method, it should be understood as a strength – in that it allows for, and encourages, a

1

continual reflection on the research activity itself. Such 'reflexive' research processes as the community or case study have the advantage of making the social world studied 'open' to others who would wish to examine the results produced. It is through such transparency of method that the research community can modify, reject, support and build upon the findings of others. Within this context the research shifted focus to examine the wider social practices of the residents of The Heath and their relationship to the use of the recreational and sports facilities. Such practices involved first, the struggle over how the facilities should be used including the appropriateness of certain activities and second the relations between those who made use of the facilities and those who did not, including the perceptions of one by the other. Here the analysis of the leisure and recreational facilities on the estate can be likened to Wild's discussion of Grange and the role of the Golf Club in Bradstow (Wild, 1978), although, at the same time, this study retains its focus on the contention that leisure or, more accurately, non-work practices are becoming increasingly important in contemporary society.

METHODOLOGY AND DATA COLLECTION

The methodology employed in any study will reflect the theoretical interests and concerns of the investigation. Yet, to assume that research methodologies lay themselves at the feet of the researcher, to be chosen solely on the grounds of efficacy or appropriateness to the investigation at hand is to disregard the varied epistemological positions associated with the discipline, and the ontological views that such positions both form and are formed by. Nowhere is this more clearly in evidence than in the distinction between qualitative and quantitative research. The former stresses the importance of an 'understanding' or *verstehende* approach in its epistemology, and an ontological view which sees human action as the principal concern of the researcher. As such research methodologies associated with obtaining an understanding of everyday life are paramount to such investigations. Ethnography, participant observation, life history and unstructured interviewing are the principal modes of data collection for such approaches. In contrast, quantitative research methods, particularly those associated with the mathematical or statistical modelling of data have tended to become associated with a sociology whose epistemological position sees human beings as operating within the constraints of institutional and organisational structures, and whose ontological view sees the examination of the relations between such structures as the researcher's prime concern (Berger, 1966; Berger and Luckmann, 1971; Dawe, 1970). This study rejects such singular methodologies and argues for what Jenkins (1983:24) has termed a 'methodological promiscuity'. Indeed given the theoretical orientation of this study, it is argued that such promiscuity is a necessary requirement of an analysis that attempts an understanding of social practices through a history of class composition and occupational restructuring, and in the context of contemporary cultural change.

The data for the study was collected in three ways: by ethnography, interview and questionnaire. The ethnography was conducted over a period of three years during which time I and my family were resident on the estate and participated in its social life including helping to staff the club for young people, playing tennis and squash, and drinking at the clubhouse bar. For many I was simply another resident of The Heath, who, because he was a sociologist, was particularly interested in what 'people got up to in their spare time'.

Initially a number of formal, structured interviews with residents were envisaged, in part to examine some of the ideas that were emerging from the ethnography. However, as the ethnography proceeded it became obvious that such interviews could be undertaken more successfully as a part of the ethnography itself. As such, unstructured, in-depth interviews were undertaken, more as conversations in a series of natural settings. Indeed, on many occasions the ethnographic work and interviews became inseparable, particularly when members of group conversations began, without any prompting, to reflect upon their own and each other's biographies.

The questionnaire was administered after most of the ethnographic work had been completed. It provided information on demographic detail, socio-economic origin and quantitative information regarding participation in leisure activities and membership of voluntary associations. In addition an assessment was made of the nature of friendship networks and sociability by asking a series of questions relating to visits to and from other households.

3

OUTLINE

One reason for expanding upon the original objective relates to developments in social theory, in particular the attempts of Pierre Bourdieu and Anthony Giddens to provide a route out of the theoretical cul de sac associated with arguments of primacy over structure and agency. On both the theoretical and empirical front Bourdieu's work has contributed much to an understanding of the stratification processes in contemporary social life, and his conceptualisation of the habitus and social practice provide a link with Giddens' concept of structuration which can be fruitfully explored. This study adopts a theoretical position closely associated with this body of work. It follows both Giddens and Bourdieu in attempting to examine the social world as created by agents located in time and space, and therefore located by, and productive of, particular sets of social practices. From a structuration position, these are seen as sometimes maintaining, and sometimes modifying, the systemic relations in which agents operate (Giddens, 1984). In addition to employing Giddens' formulations of structure and system, the analysis employs Bourdieu's concept of the 'habitus' in order to 'place' the varying social practices of agents in a wider social order. This approach is considered elemental in attempting to understand not only the varying social practices observed but also their cultural origins and the importance of the latter to social mobility.

Having re-focused initial intentions, and having already been engaged in participant observation work, it soon became apparent that those being studied occupied a place in the stratification hierarchy that was relatively under-researched, at least as far as empirical work is concerned. Following this introduction Chapter 2 examines some of the more pertinent work on the emergence of the new middle class in British society. Briefly stated these are, first, that oriented around Goldthorpe's *Social Mobility and Class Structure in Modern Britain* (1987); second, what are termed 'realist' or 'relational' conceptualisations of class, and the debate that includes and surrounds both these and Goldthorpe's work (Crompton, 1993); third, that part of a 'post industrial society' thesis (Bell, 1974) that argues for a changed relationship between work and leisure.

In the review of Goldthorpe's work attention is paid to examining a number of different positions that have been developed from both neo-Marxist and Weberian perspectives. The discussion focuses on the extent to which social mobility can be seen as having been essentially created through the development of credentialism, or whether other factors also need to be examined. Such a discussion is considered particularly important in any attempt to explore the degree of homogeneity associated with the new middle class especially in attempting to examine the cultural practices of such a group(s).

While a number of authors including Goldthorpe (1982, 1987, 1995), Abercrombie and Urry (1983), Savage *et al.* (1992) and Butler and Savage (1995) have commented upon the rise of a service class, have statistically documented its emergence in British society and have written of its significance with respect to capitalism in the late twentieth century, few have conducted empirical work on the everyday lives of its members. Others have made important contributions in suggesting what such investigations might consider at the cultural level, notably Lash and Urry (1987) and Featherstone (1987). In *The End of Organised Capitalism* Lash and Urry develop a thesis that suggests that contemporary western societies have entered a period significantly different to that which previously characterised them as industrial societies. They argue that considerable de-industrialisation has taken place in the western world over the past twenty years, and that this has been accompanied by significant changes in social organisation. Their book examines the decline in what they term 'organised capitalism' and the associated demise of an industrial economy together with the ordered, stable and regulated relations between the trade unions, employers and the State. It looks towards a future centring on an increasingly deregulated, largely service economy, in which a flexible labour force, volatile capital flows and state 'withdrawal' from regulation characterises 'disorganised capitalism'. In Chapter 9 of their book they examine some of the socio-cultural implications of their claims and point towards the emergence of the new middle class as providing a challenge to the traditional cultural practices of the old bourgeois.

To the extent that the subjects of this study might also be seen as a part of a new middle class or service class, it can also be seen as a case study that attempts to say something about a set of wider social processes associated with contemporary socio-economic and cultural change. However, this study is not exclusively focused on such a service class as has been documented, but rather on a socially mobile class fragment, not all members of which have achieved their current socio-economic positions through 'credentialism', that form of capital, to borrow a term from Bourdieu, most effectively obtained through higher education by the new middle class. Indeed, the extent to which a distinguishable service class can be identified, with regard to occupational activity, educational qualifications and cultural homogeneity, is the orienting theme of this study.

The setting is introduced in Chapter 3 where it is argued that The Heath can be seen as an example of the 'new countryside' produced by the spatial restructurings of a changing social structure (Relph, 1976; Gregory and Urry, 1985; Thrift, 1989) and an economic re-orientation from production to consumption (Saunders, 1986; Thrift and Williams, 1987). As such it is argued that the relationship to and identification with The Heath by its residents is problematic when considered in any traditional rural-urban context.

Following the community studies tradition the day-to-day lives of the population are examined, recording the way in which these daily experiences are structured and exploring the ways in which these experiences are made meaningful. The study documents the nature of the occupations in which residents are employed, together with the leisure practices that they construct and the extent to which such practices are related to their working lives. It considers the nature of the place in which they live and the way in which the 'sense of place' they have constructed relates to the work and leisure activities in which they engage.

The analysis of socio-structural characteristics includes features such as social origin, occupational status, educational level, age, gender and geographical mobility. The picture presented is of a new middle class of young/middle-aged 'nuclear' families. Many are highly educated and the majority of men are employed at the higher reaches of the occupational structure in managerial and professional occupations. Having established the theoretical concerns of this work in the previous chapter, this examination of the demographic structure and social origins of residents lays the foundation for further analysis of the relationships between these variables.

This is undertaken in Chapter 4 with particular reference to Bourdieu's conceptual schema of social practice, the habitus, economic and cultural capital (1977, 1984, 1985). Here an attempt is made to locate Bourdieu's work alongside the 'realist' position in the work of Abercrombie and Urry (1983), Lash and Urry (1987), Savage *et al.* (1992) and Butler and Savage (1995). Further analysis of the quantitative data shows that education, social origin and gender provide important distinguishing characteristics, and that these are further compounded when occupations are examined. Rather than an homogenous social grouping based on 'credentialism', the results suggest that it is heterogeneity that characterises the new middle class.

In Chapter 5 patterns of sociability are examined and the role of leisure in the social construction of identity is analysed. Particular attention is given to the social practices associated with the use of the recreational facilities available on the estate, the creation and membership of a variety of clubs and associations, and the diversity of residents' leisure lifestyles. The concern is to discover the extent to which the heterogeneity uncovered in the previous chapter can be related to residents' leisure practices and to examine further the contention that social position amongst the new middle class is best understood as being formed from processes associated with consumption rather than production. The analysis finds important differences in the 'leisure lifestyles' of residents according to social background, education and occupation.

The domestic household is examined in Chapter 6, and gender differentiations are analysed. With respect to Goldthorpe's work a number of writers (Crompton, 1989) criticise the failure to explore the role played by females in the occupational structure and the effect that this may have on class location. Further, given the radical changes associated with the move towards service industries and the relative decline of heavy manufacturing industry, together with the increasing paid female labour force, it is argued that dual incomes may be an important feature of social mobility for some of the new middle class.

It has been suggested elsewhere (Edgell, 1980) that if the concept of the conjugal role has any validity, then it will be amongst the middle classes where traditional divisions of labour are most likely to begin to disappear. Edgell's work was unambiguous in its refutation of this thesis. Similarly, recent work in the sociology of leisure (Deem, 1986; Green, Hebron and Woodward, 1987 and 1990) has also argued that the domestic division of labour effectively reduces women's experience of leisure. The evidence from this study supports the thesis that much of women's leisure can be considered 'secondary' and replicates, for the most part, the domestic divisions of labour discovered in other studies. At the same time it is argued that differentiations do exist, that they relate to those differences previously discovered and that they provide further evidence for the cultural fragmentation and heterogeneity of the new middle classes.

Chapter 7 presents the findings of the observational work conducted at the clubhouse on The Heath, which contains the sports and leisure facilities and acts as the principal public site for interaction amongst residents. The distinctions observed in the earlier chapters are contextualised within the ethnography of the clubhouse site. It is argued that it is the 'practices of use' (Bourdieu, 1984; de Certeau, 1984) of these facilities and, of course, their non-use, which help residents to position themselves and each other, within the setting. As such, the leisure practices outlined are practices by which these class fractions announce and establish their positions, and they reflect the positions of these class fractions in the changing economy.

In reviewing the study we argue that the structural and cultural fragmentation of the middle class is best understood not solely as productive of a 'new middle class' but rather as a process that has implications for the very concept of class itself. In this context our argument is not that social mobility has simply made the middle class 'larger' but that it has destroyed many of the common elements previously possessed by, or understandable as, the middle class. In relating these findings to the relationship between the concept of class and contemporary theorising (Giddens, 1991; Beck, 1992; Lash and Urry, 1994) it is suggested that some of the processes illustrated in this case study indicate a more complex cultural transformation than can be understood simply as a recomposition of the middle class.

2

LOCATING THE NEW
MIDDLE CLASS

Chapter 2 provides an overview of some of the more pertinent
work on the emergence of the new middle class in contemporary
British society and is primarily oriented around the debate concerning the relationship between changes in the class structure
and changes in the occupational structure as they pertain to social
mobility (Goldthorpe, 1987). Here the intention is not to claim or
offer this case study as a contribution to that debate as such but
rather to review contemporary work in this area and comment
upon its relevance to this project.

Clearly one could not hope to provide a definitive examination
of the considerable variety of opinions regarding the changing
nature of the British class structure. Recent authoritative work
that reviews the many competing claims has been completed by a
number of authors, notably Goldthorpe (1987) and Crompton
(1993). By way of an introduction to our own concerns we can
note those claims that relate to a changing class structure, social
mobility and occupational change. The ideas of particular interest
are fourfold. First, the amount and degree of social mobility in
Britain since the 1950s. Second, the competing explanations of
such mobility. Third, the degree to which changes in the occupational structure can be used to formulate explanations of
change within the class structure. Finally, the degree of fluidity
and openness in the contemporary class structure.

There is a consensus among writers concerned with these areas
that the contemporary occupational structure of British society
has undergone profound change, and that this change can be
characterised by an increase in non-manual, white-collar and service occupations and a decrease in blue-collar, manual occupations. It is here that the agreement ends; in accounting for and

commenting on such change a variety of competing explanations are offered which have their origins in classical social theory. For the most part such debate has centred on two related issues. First, the extent to which occupational change has affected the class structure and problematised particularly Marxist but also Weberian theory (Bottomore, 1965; Braverman, 1974; Giddens, 1973 and 1981; Goldthorpe, 1987; Roberts *et al.*, 1977). Second, the appropriate conceptualisation of a new middle or service class and its potential for either fragmentation or homogeneity (Goldthorpe, 1982, 1987 and 1995, Roberts *et al.*, 1977; Abercrombie and Urry, 1983; Lash and Urry, 1987; Savage *et al.*, 1992; Butler and Savage, 1995). Of course, to account adequately for such work would require more space than is available here but an understanding of these debates is essential if we are to make sense of the emergence of the new middle class.

CLASS AND THE OCCUPATIONAL STRUCTURE

The principal concerns expressed can be summarised by examining some of the more prominent contributions to these debates. Such contributions would include, first, what has come to be known as the 'buffer zone' thesis expounded by Bottmore (1965); second, the 'closure' thesis associated with the work of Parkin (1979); third, that associated with the Oxford Social Mobility Group (Goldthorpe, 1987); fourth, that of 'proletarianisation' and 'deskilling' developed by Braverman (1974); fifth, the work associated with notions of 'credentialism' and argued by both Urry (1981; Abercrombie and Urry, 1983) and Giddens (1973); and finally, the thesis of 'pluralist fragmentation' developed by Roberts *et al.* (1977).

Of course not all of the above positions are mutually exclusive and it would be wrong to associate any one author's view with a singular thesis, or indeed any one thesis with a singular author. However, for the purpose of clarity I think it is reasonable to suggest that certain writings could be said to be characterised primarily by one or more of the above perspectives.

The buffer zone thesis

The buffer zone thesis argues that, in spite of the movement from an occupational structure based on a manual/non-manual divide to one that has seen the growing emergence of non-manual work at the expense of manual work, the social mobility that has taken place will be of primarily short-range. In this view of the occupational structure the offspring of manual workers, while they may find themselves in non-manual work, will be employed at the lower rungs of the non-manual work hierarchy. As such, although working conditions, pay and other work related features may have improved in comparison to those enjoyed by manual workers, such improvements will have been relatively slight. The buffer zone between manual and non-manual work operates in such a way as to limit social mobility and, as Goldthorpe points out,

> it proposes the division between manual and non manual occupations as a fundamental line of cleavage within both the occupational hierarchy and the class structure, and as one which is of major importance in preventing mobility of a long range kind.
>
> (Goldthorpe, 1987:48)

Such a position has become almost a truism in theorising social stratification and can be discovered unchallenged in the work of a number of authors including Giddens (1980) and Parkin (1979). Both offer Miller's analysis of comparative social mobility (1960) in suggesting that movement between the manual and non-manual sector is of relatively short-range.

> We could sum up these remarks by suggesting that there is what might be called a social and cultural 'buffer zone' between the middle class and working class proper. Most mobility, being of a fairly narrow social span, involves the movement into and out of this zone rather than movement between the class extremes.
>
> (Parkin, 1979:56)

> It will suffice to emphasise here that the division between non-manual and manual labour in terms of inter- and intragenerational mobility, continues to be, through the operation of the 'buffer zone'.
>
> (Giddens, 1980:199)

After an analysis of the data collected, in which both inter- and intragenerational mobility were examined, Goldthorpe concludes,

11

Our findings appear as a conspicuous exception to the argument advanced in expounding the buffer zone thesis that 'it is very generally the case ... that the chances of intergenerational mobility out of the working class are heavily concentrated within the skilled manual category'.

(Goldthorpe, 1987:48)

and later,

Our own conclusions would be that attempts to comprehend currently observable mobility flows and their implications for class formation in any way which can be summed up in some simple metaphor (the buffer zone thesis) are unlikely to be very enlightening.

(Goldthorpe, 1987:55)

Class and closure

The essential argument behind the closure thesis is that social practices engaged in by those occupying the highest positions in the stratification hierarchy are employed in order effectively to close recruitment to those positions from below. Such an argument was originally advanced by Bottomore in both *Classes In Modern Society* (1965) and *Elites In Society* (1966), and similar positions have been offered by others. More recently it is in the work of Frank Parkin where this thesis has been expounded. He presents the essence of the thesis thus:

In modern capitalist society the two main exclusionary devices by which the bourgeoisie constructs and maintains itself as a class are, first, those surrounding the institutions of property; and second, academic or professional qualifications and credentials.

(Parkin, 1979:47)

Yet after examining the 'inflow' of males to the highest positions in the occupational hierarchy from his own data Goldthorpe is led to conclude,

For our present concern, what is immediately striking in Table 2.1 is that, directly contrary to any notion of closure at the highest levels of the class structure, Class I of our schema displays, on any reckoning, a very wide basis of

12

recruitment and a very low degree of homogeneity in its composition.

(Goldthorpe, 1987:44)

Of course one could easily point to a number of problems with respect to this analysis. First, that the degree of refinement of the scale employed by Goldthorpe is inadequate, in that those writers referred to above are primarily concerned with an analysis of elites existent within Class I which Goldthorpe takes to be the elite class. The argument would be that while Class I *contains* the elite class, it *does not* represent that class. Second, Goldthorpe's analysis does not in itself refute the closure thesis. Social practices of closure may well operate in the recruitment to Class I but, due to particular demands over a relatively short run period, recruitment into Class I has been 'opened' but may in the future 'close' again. Third, the closure strategies employed may, again over a relatively short period, have been inadequate to prevent a degree of long-range mobility. Future strategies of closure may prove to be more successful. What is interesting with respect to the closure thesis is the extent to which we may witness alternative strategies of closure which respond to the changing nature of the occupational system as manufacturing and primary industrial activity gives way to an economy with a greater reliance on a service sector, high technology industries and intellectual capacity than ever before. Indeed, the examination of cultural practices amongst what Roberts *et al.* (1977) have termed the fragmentary middle mass may well reveal the formation of 'closure' practices as competing social groups attempt to maintain the positions that they currently occupy. Of course such strategies are directly implicated in the formation of classes or what Giddens has termed, class structuration.

> The major problems in the theory of class, ... do not so much concern the nature and application of the class concept itself, as what, ... I shall call the *structuration* of class relationships ... to focus upon *the modes in which* 'economic' relationships become translated into 'non-economic' social structures.
>
> (Giddens, 1980:105)

Goldthorpe and social mobility

While for Parkin, 'Strategies of exclusion are the predominant mode of closure in all stratified systems' (Parkin, 1979:45), for Goldthorpe,

> there is in fact no possibility of service-class positions in present-day British society being largely confined to men of service class origins: rather, some substantial degree of 'recruitment from below' has been inevitable although very wide inequalities exist in chances of access to the service class, in particular as between men of service-class and working-class origins, this still does not prevent the latter from forming a large component of all service-class entrants.
>
> (Goldthorpe, 1987:331)

Goldthorpe's discussion of the new middle class, understood primarily as a 'service class', focuses on the extent to which social mobility can be seen as having been essentially created through the development of credentialism or whether other factors also need to be examined. Such a discussion is particularly important in any attempt to explore the degree of homogeneity associated with the new middle class especially in examining the cultural practices of such a group(s). Goldthorpe provides considerable evidence to indicate that a substantial amount of social mobility is not the result of a growing credentialism in British society and indeed argues that

> The rate of expansion of the service class in modern Britain, outstripping that of the institutions of higher education at least until the later 1960s, has meant that indirect routes into service-class positions have remained of considerable importance up to the present day.
>
> (Goldthorpe, 1987:333)

However, his concern with developing the concept of a 'service class' leads him to suggest that credentialism is in the process of becoming the dominant factor in structuring class relations.

> the last half century or so has witnessed in Britain not only a significant expansion of professional, higher technical, administrative, and managerial positions; but

14

further, the emergence of the service class as a new social formation: that is, as a collectivity of individuals and families that maintains its identity as a class – its location within the structure of class positions – over time ... its members, despite their diverse origins, display a high degree of both intergenerational stability and work-life continuity.

(Goldthorpe, 1987:333)

While such a prediction may be correct, given his own emphasis on the amount of social mobility that cannot be accounted for by credentialism it is perhaps warranted to consider alternative scenarios – scenarios acknowledged by Goldthorpe himself,

Another consequence of the growth of the service class has been that structural divisions within it – in terms say of *situs* or sector or occupational groupings – have become more apparent, and this, it should be noted, has also prompted speculation on possible socio-cultural, and political diversity.

(Goldthorpe, 1987:341)

Of course, any analysis aware of the importance of historical and economic factors in the structuration of classes would recognise the possibility of alternative scenarios to that implicit in Goldthorpe's account. The reliance on credentialism as the singularly favoured explanatory factor could be said to be more accommodative of the industrialisation thesis than of any other explanation of social change to the extent that it sees the development of technology as the driving force, requiring an ever-increasingly educated work force. Only if credentialism is seen as one strategy employed amongst others can it be understood in any historical context, and, as Parkin (1979) has argued, credentialism is a peculiar strategy to embark upon given the competition it produces for places, even though the educational system favours members of this social group.

Fragmentation

In *The Fragmentary Class Structure* Roberts *et al.* (1977) are primarily concerned with examining people's images of class according to the relative positions that they occupy, and the relationships

15

between occupation, politics, education and class consciousness. Their main conclusion from this analysis is that the changes that have taken place in the occupational structure do not evidence processes of either embourgeoisement (Zweig, 1961) or proletarianisation (Braverman, 1974).

> contrary to immediate post-war fears, far from declining, the middle class has grown in size as the development of the economy has created new white-collar jobs in the professions, administration, management, science and technology. Since the nineteen-fifties it has been more common to hear claims that we are becoming a middle class society. But in the process of growing the middle class has become a different type of social formation than the middle class with which Lewis and Maude (1949) sympathised . . . They were men of substance and independence who represented an ideal that other persons . . . could admire and emulate. No one who has examined the middle class during the last twenty years has used these as representative figures. There has been general agreement that the middle class is changing. But in what direction? And is it any longer possible to identify a core middle class culture comprising a coherent set of values and an associated style of life?
>
> (Roberts et al., 1977:107)

They suggest that we are witnessing an increasing fragmentation of the class structure based on an emergent 'middle mass' whose market and status can be differentiated in four ways. First, those employed in large organisations similar to those examined by Whyte (1956), although, significantly, such employees are characterised very differently from those in the Whyte thesis. Whereas Whyte characterises such employees as being on a treadmill – embarked upon a rat race – Roberts et al. suggest that today's 'organisation man' is more concerned with his family and extra-work activities than his career. Second, a white-collar, low skill level, clerical grouping appropriate, in part, to Braverman's analysis of an increasingly deskilled, proletarianised labour force. Third, a traditional middle class *petite bourgeoisie*. Finally, a professional, upwardly mobile group of 'credentialists' (Goldthorpe, 1987; Urry, 1981; Abercrombie and Urry, 1983).

16

This picture of the shape of the class structure has much to commend it. It recognises the decline in manufacturing and primary industries in which traditional working-class communities were found and it recognises the importance of geographical mobility, educational opportunity, technological change and the growth of white-collar trade unionism among the factors that have contributed to the decline of the traditional class structure and the emergence of an increasing heterogeneity. In spite of presenting a picture of increasing heterogeneity, the fragmentation that it suggests is one that relies on what could be described as a vertical model or hierarchy of occupations which clearly distinguishes one grouping from another.

> our interpretation of the evidence suggests that ... Within the white-collar strata ... The days when it was realistic to talk about *the* middle class are gone. The trends are towards fragmenting the middle class into a number of distinguishable strata, each with its own view of its place in the social structure.
>
> (Roberts *et al.*, 1977:143)

In this model social mobility is still primarily understood as achieved by a growing credentialism, which, although it favours the traditional middle class, had allowed for social mobility amongst working-class youth in the 1950s and 1960s to the extent that (a) they did well at school (the working-class grammar school boy), and (b) the expansion in non-manual work *required* entry into these new 'middle mass' occupations. As such, experience of social mobility is primarily understood as short-range, with a series of closures at the varying levels of an emerging, fragmentary class structure. Such a picture, although clearly presented, does not allow for the range of mobility discovered by both Goldthorpe (1987) and Payne (1987), whose findings are also supported by our, albeit limited, data. Importantly, particularly for the argument that follows, this fragmentation thesis allows for the emergence of a new middle mass, fractions of which may well express a variety of alternatives concerning cultural life, attitudes to work, domestic life and leisure. However, the problem with the formulation provided by Roberts *et al.* is their presentation of these alternatives in a pre-given hierarchy based on occupational position, rather than as potentially

17

contradictory cultural forms, the hierarchical outcome of which is continually struggled over.

REALIST AND RELATIONAL POSITIONS ON CLASS

In *Mobility and Change in Modern Society* (1987) Payne argues that much previous work on social mobility has failed to differentiate between changes in the class structure and changes in the occupational structure. The essence of his argument is that in much sociology, particularly empirical work, social class is inevitably understood in terms that relate it to a series of placements in the occupational structure.

> Social or 'class' mobility is normally thought of as a movement between social classes, whereas it is often operationalised in occupational terms and what is actually measured is movement between broad groupings of occupations. It is therefore often forgotten that social mobility is in fact occupational mobility, and so it is a product of employment processes which have taken place in specific historical and economic circumstances.
>
> (Payne, 1987:ix)

In principle, when operationalising the concept of class, occupational divisions are created by investigators and can be as complex or as simple as is seen fit. For the most part the divisions that are operationalised tend to relate to *manual labour* – unskilled, semi-skilled and skilled – and *non-manual labour* – clerical, administrative, professional and managerial. The working class is inevitably defined through the former categories, the middle class through the latter. From a Marxist position, and in spite of attempts to understand class as a relational concept, when empirical data is examined, it is usually done so with reference to location in the occupational structure for those under scrutiny. As such, the debate over the existence or otherwise of a new middle class is reduced to the task of claiming the *petit bourgeois* or service worker as a member of either a proletariat or a bourgeoisie.

Membership of the proletariat is claimed as a form of self-employed labour aristocracy or as workers involved in the means of mental production or even as non-productive workers, in the sense that they are seen as a drain on surplus value rather than

18

creators of it. Membership of the bourgeoisie, on the other hand, is usually argued for either in terms of any self-employment status constituting ownership of the means of production or in terms of the identification of certain non-manual workers' 'class interest' as lying closer to that of the bourgeois in capitalist society. Such analyses, for the most part, produce a view of contemporary British society in which *closure* rather than *openness* is seen as best fitted to explaining the occupational *and* class system. In contrast, the industrialisation thesis views the changes associated with movement from manual to non-manual work as evidencing social fluidity characteristic of an *open* structure.

Such analyses are problematic on a number of counts but especially so because of their implicit failure to operationalise adequately the concept of class in relational terms, to adopt a more historical approach to class formation and to recognise the inappropriateness of an attempted understanding through the occupational structure, which class relations could themselves be said to have produced. Such production or, for Giddens, structuration can be evidenced in a variety of ways, but would include the social practices of collective struggle, the development of credentialism and professionalisation, and the continued creation of new occupations such as, most recently, those developed through high technology, including computer personnel and technicians of various kinds. To claim that such occupational change results from the logic of capitalism or the development of industrial society says little of the relations between employers and employees, the trade unions and growth of professional associations, of changes in occupational culture, of the developing relationship throughout the twentieth century between education, training and professionalisation and, finally, of the competing claims, resources of and struggles between each and all of the above. In short such claims say little of the *specific historical* and *economic circumstances* productive of such change.

Any analysis of the social group(s) currently understood as the new middle class or service class therefore requires its historical emergence to be accounted for, not in order to place it (ultimately) as part of a proletariat or bourgeoisie, but rather to consider its emergence as a class structured by the mediation of particular socio-economic and historical circumstances (Thompson, 1963;

Stedman-Jones, 1983; Przeworski, 1985). A similar position is taken by Wacquant when, after reviewing the 'boundary problem' associated with the middle class, he states,

One cannot understand class structure (i.e., the bases and forms of interclass systems of material and symbolic relations) without, at the same time, understanding class formation (intraclass relations). Therefore, we must forsake the essentialism implied in the will to decide in abstracto, by pure theoretical fiat, what group is what and where its 'boundaries' lie groups and boundaries are made and unmade in history, not in theory.

(Wacquant, 1991:51)

Such analysis, what has been termed a 'realist' analysis (Crompton, 1993:42–45), has been developed by Urry and others (Abercrombie and Urry, 1983; Lash and Urry, 1987; Bagguley et al., 1989; Savage et al., 1992). This form of analysis has been characterised by Bagguley et al. thus:

Realist models of the social world distinguish between relatively enduring social entities which have causal properties, and specific, contingent events to which the social entities give rise. The relations between causal entities are highly complex, however, in that the realisation of their causal properties is not guaranteed but often depends upon the realisation, or partial realisation, of the causal properties of other entities; or, indeed, upon the blocking of the realisation of the causal properties of other entities whose effects may otherwise be contrary. The way in which empirical phenomena arise, then, reflects the intricate relations between entities, with the mutual realisation, part-realisation or blocking of their causal powers.

(Bagguley et al., 1990:3)

This socio-historical approach informs Abercrombie and Urry's, *Capital, Labour and the Middle Classes* (1983) in which the development of the service class (Goldthorpe, 1982; Lash and Urry, 1987) is understood to have had a destabilising element within contemporary capitalist society.

in modern capitalist societies the 'causal powers' of the service class have become significantly enhanced – powers reflected in various kinds of economic, political and social struggles which have increased the development of the socialisation of unproductive labour, forced mental and manual labour further apart, increased the credentialisation of both places and persons, concentrated capital functions within the service class, deskilled the white-collar labour process, separated the service class from deskilled white-collar workers in respect of their market and work situations, and transformed the political position of labour. They have, in other words, transformed the very structure within which the service class is to be seen as a 'class-in-struggle'.

(Abercrombie and Urry, 1983:153)

In contrast Goldthorpe sees the service class as 'a primarily conservative force within modern society, so far at least as the prevailing structure of class inequality is concerned.' (Goldthorpe, 1987:341).

Whereas Lash and Urry (1987) contend that the service class can be seen to be an important driving force behind contemporary cultural and political change, Goldthorpe has recently restated his original view that the service class can be understood as essentially conservative.

Members of the service class, occupying, as they do, the more rewarding and generally desirable positions within the social division of labour, are unlikely to be attracted to movements or parties that uphold egalitarian values or policies, but will rather seek to preserve the status quo within which their positions of relative power and advantage are established.

(Goldthorpe, 1995:322)

Savage et al. (1992a) is also informed by a socio-historical, realist approach. The concern with middle-class formation, and the analysis of the middle classes' access to 'assets' – the 'property, bureaucracy and culture' of the title, can be seen as hallmarks of such an approach.

To anticipate and simplify, we see middle class formation as being based around three causal entities: property, bureaucracy and culture. These are not symmetrical in the properties they possess, and indeed much of our argument rests upon the differences between these three assets: organisations do not convey the same degree of security as cultural assets, while cultural assets can only be effective in allowing exploitation when used in organisations or enterprises. Property assets, however, are more robust in conveying exploitative potential. However it is central to the realist argument that causal properties are only activated in certain contingent conditions. We cannot assume that, because there are three different assets affecting middle class formation, people can be neatly slotted into one of three middle classes, each with different attributes. Classes are only formed in particular historical and spatial circumstances, and an elaboration of these is vital to show how middle classes actually emerge as distinct social collectivities.

(Savage *et al.*, 1992a:xiii).

Although the emphasis on contingency and multidimensionality of the realist approach can be understood as a source of both strength and weakness, it must be recognised that the approach has provided a rich source of material in recent years (Keat and Urry, 1982; Abercrombie and Urry, 1983; Lash and Urry, 1987; Bagguley *et al.*, 1990; Savage *et al.*, 1992).

The realist approach has sometimes resulted in a certain vagueness which 'takes everything into account' *therefore* . . . it is difficult to provide empirical tests of association and causal relationships . . . However, the realist approach is a flexible one and has provided a number of important insights into contemporary social developments.

(Crompton, 1993:45; my emphasis)

The approach also lies easily alongside the work of Giddens (1987) and Bourdieu (1984) in terms of both the analysis of potential fragmentation within notions of contingency and multidimensionality – linking to Bourdieu's conceptual schema of the 'capitals' and 'habitus' – and the emphasis on processes of formation – linking to Giddens' differentiation of structure and system, and Bourdieu's emphasis on social practices. Bourdieu's work operates with a quite distinct definition of class in which cultural factors are seen to operate alongside economic ones with primacy given to neither. In this regard his work could be said to echo that of Thompson (1963) who argues against economic determinist or structuralist explanations. However, while Thompson was undoubtedly a significant contributor to the 'culturalist-action' thesis versus the 'economic-determinist' thesis, a debate held within Marxist theory in the 1960s–1970s, Bourdieu's work sits uneasily within this debate. Rather he may be best seen as developing a position that denies primacy to structure or action. As Wacquant has indicated in discussing Bourdieu's work,

> The work of Pierre Bourdieu (1978, 1979, 1984a, 1988) exemplifies this shift from abstract theorizations of 'objective' class boundaries flowing from economic structures to a focus on the structured formation or self-production of class collectivities through struggles that simultaneously involve relationships between and within classes and determine the actual demarcation of their frontiers. Bourdieu replaces the concept of class structure with that of social space, understood as the multidimensional distribution of socially effective forms of power (or capital, be it economic, cultural or social) underlying social positions. To speak of social space, he says, means that 'one cannot group anyone with anyone while ignoring fundamental differences, particularly economic and cultural ones. But this never entirely excludes the possibility of organizing agents in accordance with other principles of division' (Bourdieu 1984a, p. 9). For social space is at once a field of objective forces and a field of struggles over the very criteria of group formation . . . In this perspective, the nature, composition and dispositions of the middle classes cannot be directly 'deduced' from an objectivist map of the class structure; their boundaries cannot be 'read off' objective (i.e., theoretical) criteria of classification. Rather, they must be discovered through analysis of the whole set of creative strategies of distinction, reproduction and subversion of all agents.
>
> (Wacquant, 1991:52)

Such a position can also be found in Giddens' development of structuration theory.

> Human agency and structure . . . are logically implicated with one another . . . Understood as rules and resources implicated in the 'form' of collectivities of social systems,

23

reproduced across space and time, structure is the very medium of the 'human' element of agency ... agency is the medium of structure, which individuals routinely reproduce in the course of their activities.

(Giddens, 1987:220–21 in Crompton, 1993:184)

For Bourdieu 'capital' is not understood solely in economic terms. Rather it should be seen as the possession of a variety of resources, the possession of which endows actors (or agents – Giddens) with the capacity to act in the social world. Such resources or capitals include for Bourdieu cultural, social and symbolic capital, in addition to economic capital. Endowment of such capital, the struggle to acquire it, together with analyses of the use to which it is put, is the defining characteristic of Bourdieu's sociology. As such the occupational structure is not understood as a concrete feature of the social world, but rather as one that is in continual flux and change. The immediate links to Giddens are obvious as are the links to notions of contingency and multidimensionality associated with the 'realist' positions of Urry, Savage and others.

This study adapts Bourdieu's concept of capital to examine social mobility and the formation of the new middle class. It compares the social and cultural practices of those of different social origin, educational level and occupation. It finds that there has been similar recruitment patterns into the new middle class irrespective of educational capital, but that those with the highest levels of educational capital have been recruited via professional employment (not surprisingly) and those with low levels have 'worked their way up' into managerial positions in manufacturing, distribution and other service occupations associated with the new middle class.

In spite of their homogeneous housing tenure and residential conditions, there are marked differences in socio-cultural life which relate to the degree of educational capital possessed, social origin, gender and occupation. Further, it is suggested that it is 'life outside of work' that acts as the main orienting feature of subjects' lives. Using Bourdieu's terminology, social origin, educational background, gender and occupation combine to form part of the *habitus* which provides a frame of reference fundamentally different to that of those who have not had similar experiences.

24

CHANGING RELATIONS BETWEEN WORK AND LEISURE

What has come to be understood as the 'post-industrial society' thesis (see below Bell, 1974; Toffler, 1970; Gorz, 1982; Touraine, 1971) and associated views regarding the 'declining importance of work' (see Kaplan, 1975; Best, 1976; Dumazadier, 1974; Kelly, 1983; Roberts, 1978) share some aspects of the themes that have informed contemporary theorising associated with a sociology of postmodern culture, particularly the relationship of postmodern culture to the formation of the new middle classes or service class (Bourdieu, 1984; Featherstone, 1987; Lash and Urry, 1987; Savage *et al.*, 1992). As we have seen, in these analyses it is increasingly consumption rather than production that is seen as the primary locator of contemporary identities. Whether this can be understood as a process occurring primarily with the emergence of a new middle class(es) or service class as outlined in that work, or whether it is symptomatic of more widespread social and economic changes in the latter half of the twentieth century (Beck, 1992; Giddens, 1990, 1991; Bauman, 1992; Lash and Urry, 1994), has been debated by those attempting empirical analyses of the implications of the 'postmodern thesis' (Sulkunen, 1992; Sulkunen *et al.*, 1997; O'Connor and Wynne, 1996; Henry, 1993). In such analyses the sociology of leisure refocuses its attention from the work–leisure couplet exemplified in the work of Parker (1971 and 1983) to examine not just other social criteria such as gender (e.g. Deem, 1986; Green *et al.*, 1990) and ethnicity (Hebdige, 1979 and 1987; Gilroy, 1987) but to problematise the very concept of leisure itself. In this reading it is suggested that traditional analyses have attempted to locate leisure practices through an understanding of their relationship to the occupational structure in which leisure, understood as free-time activity, is then 'read off' from the subjects' occupations.

In British sociology perhaps the most well-known theorist of this position has been Stanley Parker (1971 and 1983). Parker's work is fundamental in relating the importance of work to an understanding of leisure practices. Indeed Parker contends that the very nature of leisure as a social construction can only be understood in relation to work. Without work there is no leisure, in the sense that the work practices of industrial society provide the counterpoint to the development of associated leisure practices. Certainly any attempt at an understanding of the emergence of modern leisure needs to recognise its emergence alongside the processes of industrialisation (de Grazia, 1962; Roberts, 1978; Clarke and Critcher, 1985; Rojek, 1995). As each of these writers have shown industrialisation brought an increasing fragmentation to everyday life resulting in an increasing differentiation in the relationship between work and non-work time. Such observations are, of course, central to the emergence of sociology itself with the fragmentation of the social, or the increasing division of labour, being a central theme of the founding fathers (Durkheim, 1964).

Parker's principal contribution to the study of leisure is his construction of a typology of work and leisure practices in an attempt to theorise the relationships between types of leisure patterns and occupations. He identifies three dominant patterns: extension, opposition and neutrality (Parker, 1971:99–110).

The extension pattern suggests a relationship between work and leisure in which the two are almost indistinguishable. The dominance of work as central to life produces a pattern of leisure practice in which work interests predominate. Parker suggests such a pattern can be associated with those whose occupational position requires the highest levels of educational achievement and professional training.

In the oppositional pattern leisure practices engaged in are in sharp contrast to those associated with work. The two sets of practices are largely distinct and work is engaged in essentially to provide the opportunity for leisure. Thus work possesses relatively little importance for such social actors, whose primary investment is in their leisure practices. Parker suggests this pattern can be associated with those whose occupational position is in the least skilled of occupations, for example factory and assembly-line work.

The neutrality pattern is offered as an explanation for those whose leisure practices are entirely independent of their work practices. In the extension pattern leisure practices become or are a part of working practices themselves. In the oppositional pattern leisure practices, although in opposition to work practices, are primarily understood or given meaning and structure by such work practices. In this third category leisure practices are understood to be independent of work practices.

Notwithstanding the feminist critique of Parker's work (Deem,

1986; Green *et al.*, 1990) as 'gender blind', a further significant deficiency is the implicit theoretical position that he takes in locating leisure as an addendum to work. As Clarke and Critcher point out,

> the model relies on a species of functionalism . . . assuming that the existence of any social pattern or activity can be explained by the function it performs . . . ultimately he is explaining leisure as a function of work.
>
> (Clarke and Critcher, 1985:20)

In addition, as Roberts has argued,

> Although work certainly influences leisure, it creates a false impression to dwell solely upon the positive relationships that can be discerned while ignoring other data. Scrutinising *all* the evidence leads Dumazedier to the conclusion that on balance the sociology of leisure has been ' . . . hampered by its derivation from the sociology of work'.
>
> (Roberts, 1978:112–113)

More recently a number of authors have developed a substantial critique of the dominant modes of investigation in the study of leisure. Underlying much of this critical work is a fundamental questioning of the very concept of leisure itself. Amongst the most vociferous of these critiques is that offered from a feminist perspective which argues that the very definition of the concept is an essentially gendered one (e.g. Deem, 1986; Green *et al.*, 1990). Here it is argued that definitions of leisure as activity counterpoint to work invariably fail to understand the relationship that most women have to both work and leisure. Numerous studies have shown that for women leisure is an essentially hidden activity (Deem, 1986; Glyptis *et al.*, 1987; Green *et al.*, 1987), hidden alongside a plethora of domesticity and household activity associated with domestic labour and child-rearing. Indeed, Deem (1986) has argued that if women wish to experience greater degrees of freedom and more opportunities for leisure then entering the full-time labour force is perhaps a starting point for it is only then that men recognise a woman's right to free time. From a feminist perspective the history of leisure is a history of patriarchy, one in which the development of free time, time free from paid labour, has been an essentially exclusive preserve of men rather than women in a capitalist labour force. As such, to the extent that such free time is time free from paid labour, Deem and others are surely correct to argue that women's experience of leisure is essentially a second-class experience.

A further challenge to definitions of leisure as free time has been established in critical theory. From a Marxist tradition a variety of authors have argued that leisure, as we understand the term today, is a concept associated with the emergence of wage labour in capitalist society. To the question, Free time – free from what? has come the response, free from wage labour. It is argued that it is with the growth of the factory and an industrialised urban proletariat that modern leisure emerges. For these writers a continuing struggle over free time and associated activities has been the history of leisure for this proletariat. Studies from a variety of traditions have documented the nature of this struggle. Socio-historical studies have provided an understanding of the 'fears of the dangerous classes' espoused by the developing bourgeois nation state. In this tradition are a number of studies documenting the legal regulation of proletarian leisure including that relating to football, drinking habits, gambling and gaming (for example, Corrigan and Sayer, 1985; Jones, 1986; Hargreaves, 1986; Walvin, 1978).

From a Gramscian or hegemonic tradition (Gramsci, 1971) other authors have pointed to the hegemony associated with the development of modern leisure. Of particular importance has been the work associated with the Birmingham Centre for Contemporary Cultural Studies (CCCS). Here, particularly under the directorship of Stuart Hall, a number of authors engaged primarily with a cultural mapping of working-class adolescent activity showed in a series of influential pieces the ways in which such activities, although regulated and controlled, acted as a form of 'resistance' to a dominant culture (Hall and Jefferson, 1976). In these studies, sometimes more explicit than others, the very concept of leisure has been subject to scrutiny. Rather than seeing leisure as an addendum to work, to be understood and analysed alongside such work, leisure itself became a central site for conflict and challenge and to be seen as increasingly important in the construction and shaping of identities (Hebdige, 1979).

This theme is taken somewhat further in Rojek's work (Rojek, 1985 and 1995). In his discussion of the development of modern leisure Rojek argues that the developing bourgeois' relationship to leisure produces a form of leisure more concerned with control of the emotions and the body than with unfettered enjoyment of pleasure. As with the neo-Marxist analysis, he too sees the development of the rational recreation movement and the creation of organisations such as the Scouts and Boys Brigade as primarily concerned with control and restraint rather than desire or 'jouissance'. Rojek then develops his argument through a discussion of the concept of modernity rather than through the neo-Marxist analysis associated primarily with the CCCS. It is through this analysis of the role of leisure in modernity and its association with bourgeois identity that we can observe the increasing importance of leisure in contemporary society.

Nowhere is this argument more developed than in Bourdieu's work, *Distinction* (1984). Basically, as Bourdieu himself states in the introduction, *Distinction* is concerned with the development of the Weberian concept of Stande or status. Bourdieu argues that social distinctions can be observed in a variety of social practices including those traditionally associated with leisure such as holiday-making, sports, reading, music, cinema and other tastes. These fields, he argues, can be examined for the degrees of cultural and economic capitals possessed by those who inhabit them, and the social positions and trajectories of such individuals can be socially and culturally mapped in society. This in itself is not particularly new or dramatic and more than one commentary has compared Bourdieu's *Distinction* with Veblen's *The Theory of the Leisure Class* (1925) given their similarity with regard to an analysis that emphasises the symbolic importance of leisure to status. However, in *Distinction* Bourdieu begins the development of a theme that has had important implications for the debates on class, consumer culture and postmodernity.

As with all attempts to encapsulate in a few pages the sometimes dense and sophisticated arguments presented, it is inevitable that any gloss over these developments is itself fraught with criticism. Notwithstanding such critique it would appear that the debate centres around attempts to understand contemporary cultural change through an analysis that develops Bourdieu's concerns with the alleged move from a social world centred on the relationships of groups, classes and individuals to the means of production, towards one in which the principal explanatory features centre on relationships to the means of consumption (see Chapter 4).

For our purposes the primary interest in this debate is the

increasing concern given to those fields of social life that lie out-side the world of work and the increasing importance given to leisure in the development of social identity. Rather than seeing the field of leisure as subsumed to and by work, essential to Parker's analysis, this approach suggests that for many work is becoming increasingly less significant in the production of social identity and that, at least for significant sections of the new mid-dle class, new value systems may be replacing those traditionally associated with the Protestant ethic.

If we relate this approach to what Roberts has termed the 'frag-mentary class structure' then we should be able to engage in an analysis of this fragmentation which relates as much to social fields outside of work and occupation as it does to those fields themselves. Furthermore, by employing Bourdieu's concepts of economic and cultural capital and operationalising them in a way that allows for an analysis related to 'trajectories of social mobil-ity' it becomes possible to analyse the degree to which these dif-ferent accumulations of capital may relate to different forms of mobility and differentiation in lifestyles. In short, it becomes pos-sible to examine the degree to which we may be witnessing the emergence not of a new middle class per se but rather the emer-gence of new middle classes and the increasing fragmentation of a traditional bourgeoisie, challenged by both forms of capital accumulation.

3

THE HEATH: SETTING AND STRUCTURE

The locale or places associated with traditional working-class community studies have largely rested on the nature of the industrial settings in which these communities existed and the corresponding occupational activities of those studied. As such the settings of these studies have tended to be taken for granted. Similarly, the suburban context of many middle-class community studies have not seen the construction of 'place' as an important factor in the study of these communities. Rather the places have acted as the backdrop in which social life has been 'played out'. This lack of reflection can be associated with the historical emergence of such communities in the developing geography of the village, town, city and suburb, broadly understood as a passage through modernisation and industrialisation, a pattern of development primarily associated with industrial or 'production-oriented' change (Thrift and Williams, 1987; Lash and Urry, 1987).

More recently, new 'communities' such as The Heath, which forms the basis of this study, have emerged not so much from an orientation to production but rather from one related to consumption (Saunders, 1986; Thrift and Williams, 1987). In part this is illustrated by the marketing of contemporary housing developments as a commodification of the countryside, offering what might be considered a 'choice' of not simply where to live but an invitation to construct a sense of place where none previously existed. Such possibilities have become increasingly available as a result of changes associated with the car and road transport infrastructure, a movement towards a service-based occupational structure and the 'lighter' industrial economy of high technology. All have contributed to a decline in

31

those communities developed around extractive industry and industrial production. In short, no longer are places as necessarily embedded in the natural resources or physical features associated with industrialisation. Just as the emergence of the great industrial cities produced a new geography of place based upon industrial production and saw the relative decline of the 'county' and 'market' town associated with an agrarian economy, so a new geography of place is emerging as extractive and productive capacities have declined and the spatial limitations of older, urban industrial districts have suffered disinvestment (Relph, 1976; Newby, 1979; Elliot *et al.*, 1988; Gregory and Urry, 1985; Savage *et al.*, 1992). This geography is associated with the 'no place' places of the satellite towns and the M4 corridor, and more recently with 'no place' places such as The Heath, the existence of which owes more to where it is not than to where it is, other than its nearness to wherever one needs to be.

CONSTRUCTING PLACE

These 'imagined communities' (Anderson, 1983; Pahl and Wallace, 1988), Thrift argues, alongside the 'creation' of heritage (Hewison, 1987), and 'consumer culture' (Featherstone, 1987), can be seen as one of the major hallmarks of the emergence of the service class.

> the countryside and heritage traditions provide images which can produce cultural cohesion in a time of rapid economic and social change ... The countryside also provides ... an imagined community of the past to fall back into when the real community of the present seems to be falling apart ... Secondly, the countryside and heritage traditions have met and blended with consumer culture. Countryside and heritage *sell* products, and in turn these products strengthen the hold of these traditions.
>
> (Thrift in Hamnett *et al.*, 1989:30)

Thrift argues that 'tradition' is also used by members of the new service class to define themselves and exclude others. By adopting such traditions they dignify themselves with the trappings of the past and gain kudos in the present – a short cut to legitimacy.

> the essential service-class character of places replete with manicured countryside and/or heritage is strengthened as more and more members of the service class move into them ... census and other figures show that, especially around London, it is the service class which is leading the urban-rural push.
>
> Thrift in Hamnett *et al.*, 1989:34)

The Heath shares many features with those new residential estates that are advertised in the 'quality' Sunday newspapers, usually set in the Home Counties 'green belt' and offering potential purchasers not a house but a home in a new 'community' close to 'thriving market towns' and within 'easy reach' of London, either by road or rail. Such developments, the builders' preferred term, are being produced in a variety of postmodern pastiches with echoes of both Georgian and Victorian styles, or occasionally with features traditionally associated with the architecture of the old counties in which they are constructed – 'Mellow Cotswold' stone, 'Kentish oast' style, or the long-sloping rooflines associated with Suffolk and Norfolk 'tithe' barns. Two-, three- and four-bedroom houses with 'every modern convenience', a choice of kitchen appliances and tiling, 'ensuite facilities' to the 'master' bedroom, double garages, patio doors and 'L shaped' living rooms are other features typically found in the houses on such estates. The names of these properties construct and evoke the idea of tradition and the rural idyll; the more popular include the Pembrokeshire, the Winchester, the Langdale and the Henley. Street names and street furniture and landscaping are also common, again evoking images of a country life – Hollow Oak Lane, Fawns Leap, the Dell and Longacre. What such developments point towards is the increasing importance of 'place' as a symbolic commodity, evoking images of a 'golden past' increasingly lost in the 'modern world'. The introductory comments from the developer's marketing brochure for the Heath amply illustrate this attempt to commodify an imagined and symbolic past.

A new concept in residential living . . .
'The Heath'

Majestic centuries old trees line the ambling lanes and foot-paths. Thickly wooded copses crown the uplands. Soft running streams and meres sleep in the hollows.

Close by stands the ancient hunting forest of Delamere from which the new village takes its name. Once the exclusive pre-serve of kings and nobles, its remaining 4,000 acres are a nat-ural sanctuary for wildlife, a truly unique feature of an environment unparalleled in its beauty.

Its 93 acres form a self-contained island wilderness . . . Bounded to the south-west and south-east by winding country lanes and to the north by open farmland, the land was originally an old country estate from which the family had long since departed. Left to reign supreme, nature had taken full advantage. Hun-dreds of mature trees, shrubs of many varieties and wild flowers of every description combined with the overgrown formal gardens and orchards to produce an almost impene-trable thicket. In such a long undisturbed environment wildlife abounded.

Such estates are marketed not so much at a 'traditional' or 'established' middle class, but rather at the new middle class of the recently socially mobile, who, in order to achieve such social mobility have often also had to become geographically mobile (Bell, 1968). These types of estates have come to charac-terise much of the contemporary private house-building pro-grammes and have created a new relationship between home and workplace and a changed relationship to time and space. The speed of modern commuting, which increasingly divorces previous relationships associated with work, community and locale, means that these factors are no longer wedded together. As Savage points out in commenting upon apparently diverg-ent trends in local labour market studies (Allen and Massey, 1988),

Those local labour markets which have seen the most rapid economic growth are normally in rural or suburban areas, and they have benefited from the movement of employment and people out of central urban locations . . . many of the residents of these buoyant local labour markets continue to work in central urban locations . . . The point here is that this evidence implies that the changes should not be conceptualised in terms of (relatively) self-contained local labour markets, but as part of the expansion of central urban labour markets.

(Savage in Hamnett *et al.*, 1989:258)

These changing temporal and spatial relationships are not lost on the developers who have used them to market The Heath:

Although occupying a peaceful, secluded setting at the end of a quiet country lane, 'The Heath' is most conveniently located for major towns and cities ... The motorway network of the North West is indisputably the finest in the country and from 'The Heath' it is possible to travel quickly and with ease across the whole region.

Part of the appeal of such developments is both their anonymity, produced by the thoughts of being one amongst many 'newcomers' and therefore 'fitting in' quite easily to an established locale, and the opportunity to 'be in at the start of something', to learn 'homemaking' together, or to have children together, etc. – the common project of the new house is shared. This newness, together with the sense of a 'return' to a mythic community life of an imprecisely designated past is represented by the developer thus:

A new residential community which offers a quality of life unsurpassed in its standards and unique in its concept ... Although the expectation of living in the 80s is necessarily more affluent, there is much to be gained by returning to the fundamental principles of life in the agricultural village communities of the last century. People today, whilst they deserve and can afford a far more luxurious lifestyle, still in a sense like to belong to a community with a positive identity and neighbourly spirit.

Amongst other factors that account for the appeal of such developments is the 'fear of the city' – an important part of contemporary life. The flight from the city first undertaken by the established middle class at the end of the last century and from which suburbia developed, is being repeated by this new middle class, as perceived dangers from crime, poor schooling and health care are seen to be the city's lot. The new residential developments are regarded as the ideal location for raising children, particularly when they include traffic management systems which ensure that motorised vehicles are separated from the immediate vicinity of the houses and play areas.

The heart of the village
Just as in the rural community of long ago the focal point was the village street, so too on 'The Heath' ... Luxurious cottage-style homes, grouped around a meandering pedestrian way, look out to pleasant grass verges, linked by a chain of shallow ornamental pools which make a most attractive feature.

The village suburbs
Gently curving roads flanked by expansive open greens, lead off into quiet, informal culs-de-sac to reveal a range of executive homes of the very highest standards ... Almost every property differs from its neighbour to give a pleasing visual variation and a strong sense of individuality. And yet ... each home blends perfectly into the magnificent landscaped surroundings of 'The Heath'.

Such estates have become the aspiration of the families of the new middle class and are rapidly turning the rural hinterlands of our cities into a 'new countryside'. As such, this construction of 'place' has become an important feature of new estate development in the hinterlands between cities and towns.

The spatial changes involved in the development of this 'new countryside' are productive of temporal changes also. Time taken to travel to work does, in some cases, add many hours to the working week and leaves this 'new countryside' devoid of much daytime activity during the week apart from those who are not in full-time paid employment, which on these 'nuclear family' estates of child-raisers are almost always women. 'Coming home' to The Heath invites residents to view their social world as demarcated between 'on' and 'off' Heath activities, an issue discussed more fully in Chapter 7.

Your place in the country

Fresh air and freedom, beautiful verdant surroundings, luxury and space, a great social scene – these are just some of the many promises of life on 'The Heath' . . . Almost certainly you'll discover your own special place in the country and decide that you belong in the new community of 'The Heath'.

LIVING ON THE HEATH

The Heath, the newly built private residential development that is the setting of our empirical investigation, is situated in mid Cheshire, within 4 or 5 miles of three market towns, 12 miles south of Warrington and 12 miles east of Chester. It is approximately 30 miles from both Liverpool and Manchester. The M6 and M56 motorways are about 5 miles from the estate. The main Liverpool–London railway line is within 3 miles, and the Chester–Manchester railway is within 1 mile of the estate. These communication networks were emphasised by the developers in their promotional materials and are always mentioned by estate agents when marketing property available for sale.

The development contains leisure facilities for the exclusive use of residents and their guests, illustrative of an increasing privatisation or 'self-servicing' of leisure associated with the social and political changes of the past twenty years, particularly those related to the role of local authorities in Britain (Bramham and Henry, 1989). Common in the USA, such developments were relatively unknown in the United Kingdom when this study was begun, although more recently a number of other residential developments have begun to incorporate facilities of the kind found on The Heath.

Construction of The Heath began in the late 1970s and from the beginning it was planned as a 'new community'. Initially both a small church and primary school were part of these plans but were not developed. The leisure facilities include common landscaping and a large 'village green' area, a 'clubhouse' containing a licensed bar, a larger meeting room and sports facilities, including a sauna, indoor swimming pool, fitness room, two squash courts and changing rooms. Adjacent to the clubhouse and alongside the 'village green' are two floodlit, all-weather tennis courts.

When purchasing property on The Heath all property owners sign a legally prescribed contract agreeing to pay an annual fee for the upkeep and maintenance of the facilities. In addition this fee supports the employment of a licensed bar steward, bar staff and cleaning staff. Overall management of the facilities is by a committee of 'trustees', elected by the residents themselves at an annual general meeting of householders. When the development was first begun the company 'paid' the fee for each of the properties it had plans to build and during this period three of its own employees who lived on the estate sat on the management committee for the running and maintenance of the facilities. When building was completed responsibility for these facilities was handed to the elected trustees.

STRUCTURAL CHARACTERISTICS

In reporting the results of the empirical study we have attempted to answer the questions 'Who lives on the kind of estate described above?' and 'What is living there like?' One way of providing an initial indication is through the data obtained from the questionnaire that was distributed to all of the households on The Heath. Here the primary concern will be to provide an overview of the structural characteristics of the sample, before embarking on a more detailed analysis of the socio-cultural features associated with life on The Heath.

The questionnaire consisted of some seventy-two questions on a variety of aspects of social life including the nature of friendships, membership of voluntary associations, where people went for entertainment and the type of holiday they took, in addition to data traditionally associated with social demography, such as age, gender, educational level, income and occupational status.

The rest of this chapter provides an overview of the results obtained from the questionnaire with regard to social origin and occupation, income, education and geographical mobility.

An indication of the social origins of The Heath's residents can be obtained by the comparison of their occupations with those of their fathers (Table 3.1). The occupational categories used were those devised by Goldthorpe and Hope (1974). This grading system is based on the Census but also uses material collected from a questionnaire and interview sample in order to categorise occupational activity more precisely. The scale was initially developed as part of a wider investigation into social mobility undertaken by the Oxford team led by Goldthorpe. In this study the scale used is a slightly revised version of the smaller 36 point categorisation developed by the Oxford team.

From the data in Table 3.1 it can be seen that although the modal category for fathers is 2, salaried professionals, the median is 15, comprising lower grade technicians. Further examination indicates that 45 per cent have fathers with occupations traditionally associated with the working class: supervisory manual, skilled, semi-skilled and unskilled manual work. The data on the current occupations of The Heath's residents shows a marked contrast between their occupations and their fathers' occupations and provides a clear indication of the levels of occupational mobility experienced. Males are located in the very highest reaches of this occupational index. Fifty per cent are located in categories 1 through to 4 below:

1 Self-employed professionals such as doctors, lawyers, accountants and architects.
2 Higher grade salaried professionals as above but also including university lecturers, company secretaries, airline pilots and town planners.
3 Higher grade administrative officials such as senior managers in large commercial enterprises and public services.
4 Industrial managers in large enterprises such as engineering and general manufacturing.

By category 10, lower grade salaried professionals such as school teachers and social workers, almost 80 per cent of the male

Table 3.1 Occupational activity

Occupation	Males (n = 217) %	Females (n = 224) %	Fathers (n = 195) %
1 Self-employed professionals	1.4	0.9	1.6
2 Salaried professionals (higher grade)	21.7	0.4	11.2
3 Administrators and officials (higher grade)	18.4	1.8	5.5
4 Industrial managers	8.3	0.9	—
5 Administrators and officials (lower grade)	0.5	—	2.9
6 Technicians (higher grade)	5.1	0.4	3.2
7 Large proprietors	—	—	—
8 Industrial/business managers (small)	14.7	0.4	6.0
9 Self-employed professionals (lower grade)	—	0.4	1.6
10 Salaried professionals (lower grade)	7.4	20.1	6.5
11 Farmers and farm managers	0.5	—	2.3
12 Supervisors of non-manual employees	—	0.9	0.5
13 Small proprietors	1.4	0.9	5.5
14 Managers: services and small admin. units	1.8	1.8	2.9
15 Technicians (lower grade)	1.4	—	5.8
16 Supervisors of non-manual employees (higher grade)	0.9	—	1.0
17 Supervisors of manual employees (higher grade)	0.5	—	2.3
18 Skilled manual (higher grade)	—	—	4.2
19 Self-employed workers (higher grade)	—	0.4	2.1
20 Supervisors of manual workers	0.5	—	1.6
21 Clerical workers, cashiers, sales	3.7	16.1	6.7
22 Skilled manual workers (intermediate grade)	0.5	0.4	2.1
23 Skilled manual construction	—	—	5.1
24 Smallholders – no employees	—	—	0.5
25 Cooks, stewards, hairdressers	1.4	0.4	0.5
26 Semi-skilled manufacturing	—	0.4	0.8
27 Skilled manual in transport	—	—	2.3
28 Shop sales and assistants	—	1.8	0.5
29 Taxi drivers, carriers, cafe owners	0.5	0.9	0.5
30 Skilled manual (lower grade)	0.5	—	3.4
31 Agricultural workers	—	—	1.6
32 Semi-skilled manual, construction/ extractive	—	—	—

Table 3.1 – cont.

Occupation	Males (n = 217) %	Females (n = 224) %	Fathers (n = 195) %
33 Semi-skilled manual, transport	—	—	4.2
34 Caretakers, guards, doormen	—	1.8	1.1
35 Unskilled manual general labourers	—	0.4	2.9
36 Semi-employed (lower grade, street vendors)	—	—	—
37 Housewives	—	—	44.6
38 Unemployed	—	0.5	—
39 Retired	—	7.8	3.6

population of The Heath has been accounted for. Clearly, a considerable amount of upward occupational mobility has taken place.

The occupations of females fall into three main categories. The most common categorization is that of housewife which was indicated by 44 per cent of female respondents. Twenty per cent have occupations in category 10, lower grade salaried professionals such as primary and secondary school teachers, social workers and civil service officers and 16 per cent in category 21 non-manual employees in administration and commerce such as clerical workers. Approximately 15 per cent of both males and females are self-employed.

Further indications of the nature of the sample can be found in the levels of income shown in Table 3.2, where almost 70 per cent of males had incomes in excess of £15,000 and 40 per cent had incomes in excess of £20,000 per annum.

Educational qualifications are clearly important for many of this population, and are suggestive of the 'credentialism' identified in the work of other authors. Table 3.3 presents the results of the question, 'What is the highest educational qualification that you obtained?'

Relatively few respondents have no educational qualifications and a similar number, 10 per cent, have not been educated beyond school certificate level. Over 70 per cent of males have educational qualifications beyond O level, and at the highest reaches almost 45 per cent have degrees and postgraduate degrees or professional qualifications. When we examine female

Table 3.2 Income

Income	Males (n = 196) %	Females (n = 130) %
Under £10,000	10.7	76.9
£10–14,999	19.9	17.7
£15–19,999	30.1	0.8
£20–24,999	18.4	2.3
£25–29,999	8.2	1.5
Over £30,000	12.2	0.8

Table 3.3 Educational qualifications

Education	Males (n = 214) %	Females (n = 215) %
None	6.5	14.4
School certificate	9.8	10.2
O levels	10.7	29.3
ONC	7.0	2.3
A levels	5.1	9.3
HNC	17.3	—
Degree	29.4	27.4
Higher degree/prof. qual.	14.0	2.3

educational qualifications, a number of differences emerge. Approximately 54 per cent of females are not educated beyond O level, compared to 27 per cent of males. Both of what might be called primarily technical qualifications, the ordinary national certificate (ONC) and the higher national certificate (HNC) are dominated by males, around three times as many at ONC level, with no women possessing an HNC qualification. Such results are not surprising and correspond to those obtained elsewhere. Although a similar number of females as males obtain degrees, 27 and 29 per cent respectively, there is a noticeable gender differentiation at the postgraduate and professional level, 2 per cent of females compared to 14 per cent of males.

It is not our intention to comment in any detail upon these gender divisions. Other writers have documented these differences in considerable detail elsewhere (e.g. Crompton and Mann, 1994). Nevertheless it is perhaps worth noting that both the 'marriage market' and 'jobs market' may play an important role in the educational qualifications of females. Three levels of educational qualification, O level, A level and degree, occurring at ages 16, 18 and the early twenties, provide 'opportunities' to leave full-time education and enter these 'markets'. To the extent that success in these 'markets' relates not only to educational qualifications but also to other factors such as 'caring responsibilities', age and geographical mobility, in some circumstances the decision to leave or 'drop out' of full-time education may not always be a solely negative decision.

During the observational work and throughout a number of interviews it became obvious that one important reason for living on The Heath for many respondents was that it is an 'ideal place to raise a family'. As can be seen from the quantitative data presented here The Heath has a large number of children living on it and the vast majority of households can be defined as nuclear families. Table 3.4 indicates the percentage of households with children in selected age groupings.

A feature commented on in previous research, initially that by Watson (1964) and Bell (1968), relates to the geographical mobility of the middle class. Bell was particularly concerned to show the differences in geographical mobility experienced by those, following Watson, termed as 'burghers' and 'spiralists'. Burghers are defined as the local middle class, established as shopkeepers and small business entrepreneurs. Spiralists refer to those professionals for whom geographical mobility is inextricably related to occupational advancement. Edgell (1980) builds upon Bell's work on 'geographical mobility quotients' to provide an indication of such mobility for the professionals which he studied. Although the data collected here does not allow for an exact comparison to be made with Edgell's work, Tables 3.5–3.8 provide a general indication of the geographical mobility of The Heath's residents.

Table 3.4 Children in selected age groups

Age groups in years	Percentage (n = 242)
Under 2	6
2–5	14
6–11	25
12–16	27
17–19	16
over 19	28

Table 3.5 Previous residence

Previous residence	Percentage (n = 248)
Local	27
North West	32
South	18
North	11
Midlands	9
Abroad	4

Table 3.5, on previous geographical location, shows that a considerable number of The Heath's residents previously lived in a variety of locations throughout the UK. Local residents, comprising 27 per cent, are those defined as previously living within a 10-mile radius of The Heath. This would include the three market towns nearest to The Heath together with a number of small villages and hamlets. The major cities of the region are included in the North West category, which is the place of previous residence for 32 per cent of residents of The Heath. Thus 41 per cent of residents come from outside the region, including 18 per cent from the south, defined loosely as south of Coventry, and 4 per cent from abroad. These latter are invariably white British returning either from the white Commonwealth or from short term employment in the Gulf States.

Without longitudinal data, it is almost impossible to give any definite indication of length of stay, and this is made even more difficult by the fact that when this data was collected The Heath had only existed for ten years. However some indication of the nature of housing tenure can be gained from Tables 3.6 and 3.7 by noting that only just over 30 per cent of households had been resident for six years or more, and 28 per cent had been resident for less than two years. While 50 per cent of residents did not expect to move from The Heath, almost 40 per cent were sure that they would be moving, and just over 10 per cent were unable to say. If these results are understood in the context of household's satisfaction with living on The Heath, over 90 per cent of households were 'very pleased' and 'liked very much' their current location, then geographical mobility could be said to be primarily driven by the nature of the main occupations of the household, primarily held by male partners/husbands (Bell, 1968).

Just how much geographical mobility is a necessary feature of social mobility is indicated in Table 3.8 which charts the number of house moves made by respondents in the previous ten years. Although the majority of households had only moved one or two times (64%), many had moved more frequently, with four or more house moves (18%) not uncommon. Indeed nineteen families (7.6%) reported that they had moved house eight times in the previous ten years! When one considers the amount of time involved in house-moving procedures this presents an indication of geographical mobility of the highest order. Invariably those households experiencing the highest number of house moves were those in which the major breadwinner had gained a series of promotions within a large, multinational company or was employed as a specialist professional abroad. For the most part these findings are similar to those obtained by Edgell (1980) in his discussion of geographical mobility and echo those of the 'spiral-ists' discovered by Bell in Swansea (Bell, 1968).

The picture presented, is one of a fairly expensive housing development, far away from any of the problems associated with

Table 3.6 Length of residence on The Heath

Length of residence	Percentage (n = 248)
0–2 yrs	28
2–4 yrs	30
4–6 yrs	12
Over 6 yrs	30

Table 3.7 Expected length of tenure

Expected length of tenure	Percentage (n = 248)
Permanent	50
Expect to move	37
Don't know	13

Table 3.8 Number of house moves

Number of moves	Percentage (n = 249)
1	34
2	30
3	19
4	6
5	4
6 + moves	8

the dysfunctions of the two major cities of the region and located, rather, in the heartland of rural Cheshire. At the same time, however, motorway connections make these cities and their hinterlands readily accessible for work. Households are primarily of the 'young' middle aged with a predominance of children, many of whom are of pre-secondary school age and are cared for by non-working mothers. The majority of men are employed in high income occupations, in middle and senior management and the professions, whereas many of those women who are employed outside the home work in lower level clerical and secretarial jobs. While educational levels partly reflect the above, it is notable that almost 30 per cent of women are educated to degree level, a feature explored in more detail below. Compared to the conditions in which they grew up, many residents have clearly experienced considerable social mobility. In comparing occupations with the occupational activities of their fathers we saw that almost half of the men came from 'working-class' backgrounds, whereas they themselves are positioned largely at the apex of the occupational scale. Thus, social mobility has been considerable for many of them. At the same time, and certainly related, geographical mobility is also high, associated with occupational promotion and an accompanying desire to 'improve' living conditions for the nuclear families that predominate in this estate.

4

THE SOCIAL SPACE OF MOBILITY

The subjects of this study are the middle class and within that social grouping a particular fragment of that class, the new middle class. They are new in both senses in which this term has been sociologically employed. First, 45 per cent of the sample are recent entrants in that they have fathers employed in skilled and semi-skilled occupational categories. Second, over 90 per cent are employed in the service industries as identified by Goldthorpe in *Social Mobility and Class Structure in Modern Britain* (1987). However, to assume that they comprise a homogenous grouping simply because of an upward trajectory (i.e. those for whom upward social mobility has been a feature of their current social positions) or because they are located in similar occupational positions (the service industries) is to ignore two important features: first, the differences involved in the acquisition of that mobility and, second, the degree of heterogeneity characteristic of the occupations in which they are employed. Failure to recognise the above points involves a failure to recognise the differing pathways to social mobility that have been taken and the potential impact of these differing pathways for leisure activity and other non-work areas of social life. Both of these deficiencies can be highlighted and illustrated by employing the conceptual framework developed by the French sociologist Pierre Bourdieu.

BOURDIEU – AN OUTLINE

It is not my intention to add yet another contribution to the vast literature that has grown up around Bourdieu's work in recent years (Jenkins, 1992; Calhoun *et al.*, 1993) but an outline of his conceptual schema is provided below. Of particular importance to this study are Bourdieu's conceptualisations of capital and class, social field, the habitus and symbolic power.

Capital and class

Bourdieu employs the concepts of capital and class in a significantly different sense to that associated with Marxist theory. Unlike Marx, Bourdieu uses capital to signify the acquisition of status which represents differing positions in a series of social fields. In Marxist theory the ownership of economic capital is the underlying factor in the analysis of a capitalist social formation, and the concept of class possesses explanatory power through the relationship of economic capital to class. As such the concept of class is objectified in Marxist theory and objectified empirically in secondary analysis. For Bourdieu, economic capital is one form of capital among others which allows for the formation of classes and class fractions (social groups). This position, which runs throughout Bourdieu's work, is perhaps most clearly stated in 'The social space and the genesis of groups'. In the introduction to this paper Bourdieu outlines his own position thus:

> Constructing a theory of the social space presupposes a series of breaks with Marxist theory. First, a break with the tendency to privilege substances – here the real groups whose number, limits, members, etc., one claims to define – at the expense of relationships; and with the intellectualist illusion that leads one to consider the theoretical class, constructed by the sociologist, as a real class . . . Secondly, there has to be a break with the economism that leads one to reduce the social field, a multi-dimensional space, solely to the economic field, to the relations of economic production, which are thus constituted as co-ordinates of social position. Finally, there has to be a break with the objectivism that goes hand in hand with intellectualism, and that leads one to ignore the symbolic struggles of which the different fields are the sight, where what is at stake is the very representation of the social world and, in particular, the hierarchy within each of the fields and among the different fields.
>
> (Bourdieu, 1985:723)

Social field

Bourdieu argues that a variety of forms of capital (the relative accumulation of resources) can be seen to exist in a variety of social fields such as those of education (educational capital), economic wealth and income (economic capital), and aesthetics and taste (cultural capital). Acquisition of such capitals within these social fields allows for the formation of social groups. Bourdieu also suggests that within social fields types of capital will also be evaluated according to the conditions pertaining in other social fields – for example the distinction between 'old' and 'new' money which distinguishes the *nouveau riche* from the traditional bourgeoisie and acts not only to indicate the source of economic capital but also carries with it a social evaluation. Similarly in the educational field while qualifications clearly count, they may count less if achieved at one institution rather than another, such as 'Oxbridge' as opposed to the 'campus universities' or indeed at any university in preference to the 'former polytechnics'.

In the analysis to be developed here these conceptualisations of capital, class, and social field will be used to examine the pathways of social mobility experienced by the subjects of the study by locating the acquisition of capitals within social fields through the operations of the habitus. Such an analysis allows us to examine the degree of homogeneity existent within the new middle class or service class.

Habitus

Bourdieu's concept of the habitus, and in particular that part of the habitus associated with an actor's past, is employed as an explanatory factor in investigating these pathways to social mobility. The habitus acts for Bourdieu as a structuring structure and a structured structure, operating as a system of dispositions both recognised and unrecognised by agents and forming the basis for action in the social world. As such the habitus, the 'backbone' of the individual's social body, supplies a set of resources and constraints; the norms and values that shape action in a way similar to processes of socialisation, but also provisive of the constitutive rules for action. It can be seen to comprise a member's knowledge both in the ethnomethodological sense and in the sense used by Giddens, who sees agents as possessing not only the practical knowledge to repair indexicality (ethnomethod-ology) but also plans, projects and a cognitive knowledge of the nature of the social practices in which they engage. For both Giddens and Bourdieu structure refers not to an external reality separate from the subject but to sets of rules and resources which allow for the production and reproduction of social systems: 'reproduced relations between actors or collectivities, organised as regular social practices' (Giddens, 1984:25).

It is this recognition of the knowledgeable agent that allows for the ethnographic analysis of social practices as being both struc-tured by and structuring of social position, and of the habitus as provisive of a classificatory schema which allows individuals to classify the social world and to be classified by others in that social world.

Symbolic power

The fourth part of Bourdieu's analytical schema relates to the relative power of individuals and social groups in ensuring that their social practices and 'definitions of the situation' are those that hold sway in any given social field. Here Bourdieu employs his concept of 'symbolic power' to indicate that definitions of reality are struggled over by social groups. As such the power of 'naming', of constituting social reality with regard to any given social field, is a power struggled over in social space.

through properties and their distributions, the social world achieves, objectively, the status of a symbolic system ... organised according to the logic of difference, differential deviation, thereby constituted as significant distinction. The social space, and the differences that 'spontaneously' emerge within it, tends to function symbolically as a space of life-styles or as a set of Stande, of groups characterised by different life-styles ... While the structure of the social world is defined at every moment by the structure of the distribution of the capital and profits characteristic of the different particular fields, the fact remains that in each of these arenas, the very definition of the stakes ... can be called into question. Every field is the site of a more or less overt struggle over the definition of the legitimate principles of division of the field ... The social world is, to a large

50

extent, what the agents make of it, at each moment; but they have no chance of un-making and re-making it except on the basis of realistic knowledge of what it is and what they can do with it from the position they occupy within it.

(Bourdieu, 1985:730–731)

As a whole this conceptual framework provides a powerful analytical tool for examining the construction of social reality. In some ways Bourdieu's position can be likened to the theoretical tradition associated with the work of Berger and Luckmann (1971), and the phenomenological tradition in sociology. Bourdieu's work also contains a strong link with the realist tradition through his location of the habitus and social practice in the objective conditions that structure everyday life. It is this dualism of structure and agency in Bourdieu's ontological position that places him more in the structuration camp than in either the traditions of a phenomenological or structuralist sociology.

In *Distinction* (1984), Bourdieu employs his conceptual schema to explain the differences observed in a variety of both ethnographic and statistical enquiries into social life in contemporary France. In an analysis of the correspondencies between variables such as income, occupation, education and residence he argues that the accumulation of social capital is differentially distributed throughout society and that the degree (type) and amount of capitals inherited or acheived can be 'mapped' on to the differentiations observed in income, occupation, education and residence. From these he produces a model of lifestyles and cultural practices related, through the habitus, to social origin and education. His threefold hierarchy of taste, 'legitimate', 'middlebrow' and 'popular', is seen to relate to social origin and educational level such that social groups or 'class fragments' will possess differential amounts of 'cultural capital', the possession and ownership of 'legitimate' taste. However, in spite or perhaps because of the authority with which Bourdieu writes, together with his comprehensive analysis of French social structure in *Distinction*, one is left with the view that Bourdieu's model says little about contemporary social change. Certainly he offers an illuminating discussion of the French *petite bourgeoisie* and the new bourgeoisie, but inevitably these remain wedded to a search for legitimacy which is confined to amassing a knowledge of, and imitating, the existing 'legitimate' tastes of the dominant class.

51

There does reside within *Distinction* a recognition of contemporary change when Bourdieu, prefacing contemporary debate around the new middle class, symbolic consumption and postmodernity in social theory, asserts that

> The new bourgeoisie is the initiator of the ethical retooling required by the new economy from which it draws its power and profits, whose functioning depends as much on the production of needs and consumers as on the production of goods. The new logic of the economy rejects the ascetic ethic of production and accumulation . . . in favour of a hedonistic morality of consumption, based on credit, spending and enjoyment. This economy demands a social world which judges people by their capacity for consumption, their 'standard of living', their life-style, as much as by their capacity for production.

(Bourdieu, 1984:310)

Here Bourdieu appears to suggest that the new service economy is productive of a new middle class which rejects the standards of an 'old' bourgeois ethic of duty and obligation in favour of a hedonistic morality based more upon enjoyment and the pursuit of pleasure.

However, as we have indicated above, his theoretical model is more comfortable in explaining social stasis than in explaining social change. Notwithstanding these difficulties, the implications of Bourdieu's scheme for the emergence of the new middle classes have been taken up by a number of authors in recent years, including Featherstone (1987, 1991), Lash and Urry (1987), Wynne (1990) and Savage *et al.* (1992). Attention has been paid to the emergence of fragmentation within the new middle class and the consequences of this for class formation and social change.

CULTURAL CHANGE AND THE NEW MIDDLE CLASSES

For Featherstone, Bourdieu's work allows for an investigation of the practices of a new *petite bourgeoisie* who can be seen to promote alternative cultural forms to those enshrined in a 'virtuous' middle-class culture and to be involved in a struggle with that traditional middle class.

52

A perspective informed by the work of Pierre Bourdieu will be developed to argue that the new conception of lifestyle can best be understood in relation to the habitus of the new petite bourgeoisie, who, as an expanding class fraction centrally concerned with the production and dissemination of consumer culture imagery and information, is concerned to expand and legitimate its own particular dispositions and lifestyle. It does so within a social field in which its views are resisted and contested.

(Featherstone in Meijer, 1987:158)

In similar vein Lash and Urry's discussion of what they term a 'postmodernist sensibility' and its link to 'new class fractions' also employs the conceptual ideas of Bourdieu.

Our central claims in this section will be that it is the developing service class which is the consumer *par excellence* of post-modern cultural products; that there is a certain 'hegemonizing mission' of the post-modern tastes and lifestyle of significant sections of this new middle class; and that there are certain structural conditions of the service class that produce a decentred identity which fosters the reception of certain post-modern cultural goods. The best way to address these points is via Pierre Bourdieu's notion of the 'habitus'.

(Lash and Urry, 1987:292)

With regard to our concerns over the emergence and constitution of the new middle class, perhaps the most pertinent to this study is that by Savage *et al.* (1992). Here Savage attends to two fundamental questions associated with the formation of the new middle class. First, the relevance of the marketing stereotypes that emerged in the 1980s pertaining to 'yuppies' (young, urban professionals), 'dinks' (dual income/no kids) and 'career women'; all suggestive of values associated with the enterprise culture, home ownership, degendering and increased social mobility. Second, the degree of fragmentation within the middle class and the extent to which economic restructuring can be seen as an explanation for the emergence of such fragmentation. This work reviews and extends the previous work of the authors, Savage (1987, 1988), Savage *et al.* (1988), Barlow and Savage (1986), Dickens (1988) and Fielding and Savage (1987), to argue that we can indeed see an increasing fragmentation of the middle class, which introduces serious doubt of its previous characterisation as a homogenous grouping based solely on the emergence and growth of 'service' occupations.

Using data from the British Market Research Bureau's 'Target Group Index' they attempt a secondary data analysis 'of consumption behaviour by the contemporary middle classes' (Savage *et al.*, 1992:104) in an approach similar to the secondary data analysis contained in Bourdieu (1984).

> it is indeed the rapidly rising professional workers who are now adopting a version of the 'healthy' lifestyle previously espoused mainly by the 'education and welfare professionals'. These seem close to Bourdieu's 'new petite bourgeoisie', except that they also include older, more established professions, and are not as economically marginal as in Bourdieu's framework.
>
> (Savage *et al.* 1992:115)

Their analysis suggests at least three distinct groups. First, public sector professionals having 'ascetic' lifestyles characterised by sport, healthy living, and high culture pursuits. Second, managers and bureaucrats with below average consumption of high culture pursuits and sports activities, and with an otherwise undistinguished consumption profile. Finally, a group identified as exhibiting the characteristics of a 'postmodern lifestyle', defined as one lacking in any organising principle in terms of the direction of taste, but rather expressing an interest in both high and popular cultural pursuits – what Lash (1990) has termed a process of de-differentiation characteristic of postmodern cultural and economic practices (see also Wynne and O'Connor, 1992).

As Crompton (1993) has noted, Savage's findings correspond broadly to those identified by Wynne (1990) in an earlier version of the analysis presented here, and offer some support for those claims of cultural fragmentation within the middle class which

> reflects the economic and spatial fragmentation within these groupings which had already been identified by those working within more orthodox frameworks of 'class analysis' (Savage *et al.*, 1988, 1992, Crompton 1992)
>
> (Crompton, 1993:182)

54

By adopting Bourdieu's line of enquiry, and employing his concepts of capital and the habitus, we can investigate the emergence and formation of social groups on The Heath by examining the extent to which their social practices differentiate them from others, allowing for a far more sophisticated analysis than one predicated upon either the statistical analysis of discrete variables or the over-reliance on actor's views of social reality. In drawing these outlines we must be aware that the recent history of class structuration in British society cannot be understood as evidencing the emergence of a new middle class whose constitution is solely based on the accumulation of educational capital. As Goldthorpe (1987:341) indicates, occupational mobility has been achieved by some through the accumulation of educational capital and by others who have not progressed via educational credentialism. The possibility of socio-cultural diversity within the new middle class has been suggested more recently by Featherstone (1991). Commenting on Bourdieu's work and its possible application to an understanding of contemporary Britain he argues,

> the new conception of lifestyle can best be understood in relation to the habitus of the new petite bourgeoisie, who, as an expanding class fraction centrally concerned with the production and dissemination of consumer culture imagery and information, is concerned to expand and legitimate its own particular dispositions and lifestyle.
>
> (Featherstone, 1991:84)

However,

> It does so within a social field in which its views are resisted and contested and within, in Britain, especially, an economic climate and political culture in which the virtues of the traditional petite bourgeoisie have undergone a revival.
>
> (Featherstone, 1991:84)

Consequently, any analysis of this emergent social grouping needs to be aware of possible fragmentation at the socio-cultural level. It is in this sense that we can employ Bourdieu's schema to investigate possible socio-cultural differentiation in the new middle class.

THE SOCIAL SPACE OF MOBILITY ON THE HEATH

In analysing the social worlds of our subjects, the concept of the habitus is employed to suggest that the new middle class(es) needs to be understood not as a single group but rather as a set of fragmented groupings, fragmented according to the different paths of social mobility followed and structured around these paths, and therefore indicative of the different habitus they possess. In addition, the relative amounts of economic and educational capital possessed can be employed in order to discover possible differentiations in social practices and cultural preferences.

In order to examine some of the possibilities outlined above, the data on father's occupation, education and income was explored using SPSS, recoded to facilitate the investigation and subjected to further analysis. Table 4.1 shows the results of recoding father's occupation into four categories:

1 'Professional and senior management'.
2 'Administrative and middle management'.
3 'Technicians, small proprietors and supervisors'.
4 'manual workers'.

As the table reveals, almost 45 per cent of our sample have fathers in manual occupations, traditionally associated with the working class.

Respondent's occupation was recoded into:

1 'Professional'.
2 'Managerial'.
3 'Technical, sales, clerical and other'.
4 'Unemployed and retired'.
5 'Housewife.

Table 4.1 Social origin

Father's occupation	Percentage (n = 192)
1 Professionals and senior managers	18.5
2 Administrative, middle managers and officials	22.6
3 Technicians, small proprietors and supervisors	15.2
4 Manual workers	43.7

The rationale for this coding scheme relates both to the occupational distribution originally obtained from the Goldthorpe–Hope classification (see Table 3.1) and to the theoretical concerns of our argument. The majority of males in the sample are employed in either professional or managerial occupations and the majority of females are employed either in professional occupations, clerical, sales and lower-level administrative work or define themselves as housewives (see Table 4.2).

Given the results obtained in Table 3.3 'highest educational qualification obtained', this variable was recoded into a threefold categorisation, 'high' 'medium' and 'low'. 'High' includes all those with degrees and post-degree qualifications; 'medium' all those with A level/ONC/HNC qualifications; 'low' all those with O level or less than O level qualifications (Table 4.3).

As with the previous variable the data on income (see above Table 3.2) was recoded into 'high', 'medium' and 'low'. 'High' incorporates all those with incomes of £20,000 or more; 'medium' those with incomes of £10,000 or more, but less than £20,000; 'low' those with incomes of less than £10,000 per year (Table 4.4).

Importantly the coded descriptions of both educational qualifications and income are less important than our examining the

Table 4.2 Occupational activity (revised)

Occupation	Males (n = 217) %	Females (n = 215) %
Professionals	31.3	21.8
Managerial	43.3	4.9
Technicians, Supervisors and other	17.7	25.1
Unemployed and Retired	8.3	3.6
Housewives	—	44.6

Table 4.3 Educational level (revised)

Education	Males (n = 214) %	Females (n = 215) %
Low	27.1	54.0
Medium	29.4	16.3
High	43.5	29.8

Table 4.4 Income (revised)

Income	Males (n = 196) %	Females (n = 130) %
Low	10.8	76.9
Medium	50.3	18.5
High	39.0	4.6

potential relationship between them and other variables, and how this may relate to other social practices of our subjects. These interrelationships are examined below in order to explore possible links.

Table 4.5 shows the effects of social origin on occupation for males. Although the results indicate that professional occupations are associated with social origin, they are less strong than might have been anticipated. Certainly the figures indicate that a sizable minority of those with origins in the working class have achieved considerable mobility. When it is remembered that entry into professional occupations is primarily guarded by educational qualifications, these results suggest that around 30 per cent of those from working-class origins have achieved this mobility through educational credentialism or the accumulation of educational capital. Entry into management is even less strongly associated with social origin with 42 per cent of those from working-class backgrounds and just under 50 per cent of those from middle-class backgrounds being employed as managers. The technicians/supervisors and other category, accounting for only 17 per cent of males in our sample (see Table 4.2), comprises mainly those from working-class and lower middle-class backgrounds and suggests evidence of some short-range upward social mobility for those from working-class backgrounds.

Table 4.5 Social origin × occupational activity (n = 183)

Social origin	Professionals %	Managers %	Techs/sales/other %
Working class	30	42	28
Lower middle class	24	48	28
Middle class	40	49	11

Table 4.6 shows the effects of educational level on occupational position. The results suggest a clear relationship between the types of occupation entered and the educational level of respondents, with professional occupations being clearly associated with graduate levels of education and general management positions being associated more with non-graduates. Almost 70 per cent of professionals have a graduate or postgraduate education (high) and relatively few professionals, 20 per cent and 10 per cent respectively, have either 'medium' or 'low' educational qualifications. In contrast, the full range of educational qualifications are almost equally represented in the management category: 'high' 36 per cent, 'medium' 34 per cent and 'low' 30 per cent.

We can extend our analysis by examining the relationships between occupation and income. Table 4.7 shows that only 35.6 per cent of those in professional occupations are in the highest income category, compared to 56 per cent of those in management. These figures suggest both the increasing importance of the management and administration of a service economy and the relative decline of the 'professional' as educational credentialism becomes increasingly related to 'specialist' occupational activities. The suggestion is that to the extent that educational

Table 4.6 Educational level (males) × occupational activity (n = 183)

Education	Professionals %	Management %	Techs & supervisors %
Low	10.6	30.3	41.7
Medium	19.7	33.7	36.1
High	69.7	36.0	22.2

Table 4.7 Income (males) × occupational activity (n = 189)

Income	Professionals %	Management %	Techs & supervisors %
Low	6.8	1.1	22.9
Medium	57.6	42.9	62.9
High	35.6	56.0	14.2

credentialism becomes associated with occupations involved in 'professionalisation' so those occupations become increasingly 'down graded' with regard to economic reward. A further factor may well be the 'feminisation' of certain occupational activities. As we have seen in our examination of respondents' occupations, Table 4.2, the professional category accounts for over 20 per cent of female occupational activity.   hummm!

Clearly statistical differences appear when we examine the interrelations between occupation, gender, education, income and social background. Such differences echo those suggestions that the new middle class, rather than being an undifferentiated middle 'mass', displays considerable fragmentation associated with social origin, educational level and occupation. Adopting Bourdieu's conceptualisation of the capitals and the habitus and employing them here, it is argued that The Heath and social relations upon it may represent *some* of the distinctions within an emergent new middle class.

Exploring trajectories

Informal interviews conducted with residents reveal the routes taken to their current occupational positions. The following comments are the result of my request for a brief picture of social background and education, and they reveal interesting differences between occupational destinations.

> it wasn't a conscious decision in the sense that I ever said I am going to become a teacher . . . but my father teaches English at . . . and while at university . . . it seemed natural, you know, to do the Cert. Ed. [post graduate teaching qualification]. That's where we met [wife] both got teaching jobs in the same area where we stayed for four years, and then moved here about two years ago. My parents are pleased but I wouldn't say that they pushed me into it or anything like that, rather it just seemed a natural thing to do, and I enjoy it, we both do, in spite of all the changes.
>
> Secondary school teacher – middle-class background and
> higher education

typical of orient!

To be honest I was hopeless at school, a real pain I suppose but I enjoyed it and got on well with some of the teachers because I was good at sports, played for all the teams. I know my parents are proud, the idea of me being a school teacher, there aren't many from where I come from. I just got fed up with the work when I left school so I did some O levels part time then got a place at training college. I'm happy enough, I get on well with the kids, it's fine.

> Secondary school teacher – working-class background and
> higher education

After leaving school I joined a foods company and eventually became a salesman, travelling an area, working in an area, around here [the North West, Liverpool and environs]. Obviously you meet lots of people doing that, different shops, different people and I decided to start my own business selling jewellery, if you can call it that! I got an old transit van and Prince [a dog] to protect the stock, bought it [the stock] with a cheque on a Friday which I knew would bounce if I didn't sell the stuff by Tuesday. So it was all over here, and the coast around Rhyl over the weekend. That's how I started and it just grew to where I am today. Even now the work's the same but it's more stable because I've got regular clients, but I still have to be there, as you've found out. I suppose it could grow but for what, employing people is different altogether, I've tried it before and unless you get the right person it can be a proper pain. No, things are good enough as they are, at least I know what I'm doing.

> Small proprietor, wholesale low cost jewellery distribution
> to small shops – working-class background and
> 'low' education

The degree was in Town and Country Planning and I joined ... straight from university. I had about four weeks' holiday after my degree, started with ... and was with them until last year. The decision to start on my own wasn't easy, but I wanted to do it because I could see all these opportunities ... I was dealing with these people for ... and knew I could do it too ... given the money we were paying out you'd only need half a dozen clients to make it work and earn far more than I was getting. Yes, it's worked, in fact I'm busier than I want to be, well I can please myself about that, it's not really a problem (time for other things such as tennis etc.). No, I'm glad I did it, new car, new house, new baby, yeah new racket too.

> Recent self-employed planning professional specialising in preparation of clients' legal work prior to application for planning permission, previously employed by medium-sized property development company – middle-class background and higher education

Night school to start with, the degree was full-time. The first job was with the Midlands (electricity generation), then we moved here five years ago when I moved to ... Most of the time I monitor dials and ensure we have the capacity we need, those figures are national and we contribute, whatever's required really, obviously to our own capacity. I've never enjoyed the shifts, I suppose you get used to it ... but I don't really, its always difficult but ... The children, holidays, standard of living, being here ... if it wasn't for the shifts I'd play even more.

> Professionally qualified electrical engineer – working-class background and higher education

Well it's a good job, it pays well, the travel is great, we have some fun, and all the perks, flights, holidays, all over the world that you only ever read about. What else could I do, no brains, well no qualifications. The shifts aren't a problem, you can always swop with someone ... it's good.

> Airline steward – working-class background and 'low' education

I'm responsible for everything that leaves ... as far as the service is concerned, not just food, all aspects of the service. I started straight from school, no qualifications really, other than a few picked up on the way ... yes, internal in that sense, just by being promoted, being good at it. Well, yes, the travel, or rather the destinations, especially if [wife] comes, but its really administrative work now, managing and planning, overall responsibility ... Well, because of the standard of living, that's why I do it.

> Airline Catering Manager – middle-class background and 'low' education

I was training to be quantity surveyor, left school with three O levels. Do you remember those adverts on the tube, the underground, 'if you can do this equation then contact us' ... It was one of those, so I contacted them and got the job, trained as a computer programmer then got into sales – right at the beginning I suppose. At first it was very good because of the commissions structure we had. Then that changed and salaries were much more predictable, and not as good as before, well they were good, but the large bonuses disappeared and the job became more of a grind, day in day out. Also the computer industry began to change with PCs, and software became more important. Three of us made the decision together, we'd planned it and shared our bonuses, pooled them together to provide some of the capital, and we knew we would have clients, from our jobs. That's it really, lots of hard work to start with, doing everything but now we specialise and plan software packages for specific areas of need, solicitors, estate agents and the like, all small businesses at first, now particular types. Oh yeah, the work's lovely, you're joking ... it's just, just work ... a particular kind of work, but work. I don't enjoy the work, although specifying a client's requirements is OK, but then you have to do it, that's the work.

Recently self-employed computer software specialist previously employed in computer sales for a multi-national computer manufacturer – working-class background and 'low' education

In an effort to explore the above comments, and to further employ Bourdieu's concepts of the capitals and habitus, Table 4.8 combines the social origin and education variables to show how these, in combination, relate to occupational position. This variable was constructed by combining social origin (father's occupation) with the educational level of respondents. Social origin was dichotomised into 1 'working class' (fathers in supervisory manual and manual occupations) and 2 'middle class'. Education level was dichotomised into 'high' (degree level and higher) and 'low' (sub-degree level). The construction of this variable produces a fourfold classification associated with social origin and educational level:

1 'Working class/low education'.
2 'Working class/high education'.
3 'Middle class/low education.
4 'Middle class/high education'.

Table 4.8 The habitus × occupation

Social origin and education level	Professionals occupations %	Management occupations %	Other occupations %	
Working class/'low' education (n = 48)	13	48	39	100
Working class/'high' education (n = 32)	56	34	10	100
Middle class/'low' education (n = 53)	22	55	23	100
Middle class/'high' education (n = 50)	50	40	10	100

In combining these variables in this way we are able to provide for some of the principle 'structuring' features of the habitus in influencing entry into certain types of occupation. Given the theoretical concerns of this investigation, the relationship between educational capital, social origin and occupation, together with the overwhelming predominance of managerial and professional employees living on The Heath, it is these two occupational categories which have been subject to analysis.

The table shows the importance of 'credentialism' or educational capital at the highest levels of education for entry into professional occupations. While only 13 per cent of those of working-class origin and 'low' education are in professional occupations, 56 per cent of working class origin and 'high' educational level are employed as professionals. Interestingly the management category is more evenly spread with regard to social origin and educational level. It can be noted, however, that 'management' is clearly the area of employment for a considerable number of those from both working-class and middle-class origins with relatively 'low' educational levels. As such it may be that a possible cultural cleavage between 'professionals' and 'managers' may exist produced by the relative amounts of educational capital possessed.

CONCLUSION

The results of these investigations are mapped in Figure 4.1 and illustrate what we can call the social space of mobility with regard to social origin, gender, income, education and occupation. The

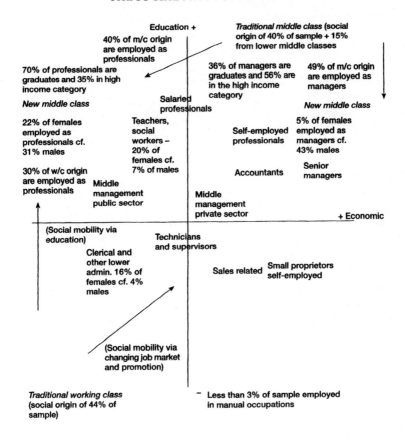

Education +

40% of m/c origin
are employed as
professionals

Traditional middle class (social
origin of 40% of sample + 15%
from lower middle classes

70% of professionals are
graduates and 35% in high
income category

New middle class

Salaried
professionals

36% of managers are
graduates and 56% are
in the high income
category

49% of m/c origin
are employed as
managers

New middle class

22% of females
employed as
professionals cf.
31% males

Teachers,
social
workers –
20% of
females cf.
7% of males

Self-employed
professionals

5% of females
employed as
managers cf.
43% males

30% of w/c origin
are employed as
professionals

Middle
management
public sector

Accountants

Senior
managers

Middle
management
private sector

+ Economic

(Social mobility via
education)

Technicians
and supervisors

Clerical and
other lower
admin. 16% of
females cf. 4%
males

Sales related

Small proprietors
self-employed

(Social mobility via
changing job market
and promotion)

Traditional working class
(social origin of 44% of
sample)

⁻ Less than 3% of sample employed
in manual occupations

Notes: (i) 44% of women described their occupation as housewife.
(ii) 54% of women are in the lowest educational category cf. 27% of men.
(iii) Men: 44% of the sample have w/c origins; 15% have lower m/c origins; 41% have m/c origins.
43% have degrees and/or professional qualifications.
33% are employed as professionals, 46% as managers, 18% as technicians and supervisors.

Figure 4.1 The social space of mobility

diagram summarizes the results above to provide an outline of
the relative social make-up of our sample. The diagram should be
seen to provide a framework around which other social practices
associated with leisure and other non-work activities in everyday
life can be understood. Clearly the diagram indicates that social
mobility from within the working class has been achieved

through both educational credentialism and promotions and other opportunities associated with an emergent service economy such as new occupations. The changed political climate of the late 1970s through to the present day will also have had an important effect on widening income differentials between occupations, particularly between those in the public, compared with the private sector. The gendered nature of occupational activities can be noted in that while 22 per cent of females are employed as professionals, compared with 31 per cent of males, only 5 per cent of females are employed as managers, compared with 43 per cent of males. The proportion of female professionals working as teachers and social workers (20 per cent) outnumbers the proportion of male professionals in these categories (7 per cent). The lowest status work, clerical and other low level administration, is also dominated by females (16 per cent of females compared with 4 per cent of males).

Figure 4.1 also provides information on the social origins of the sample, showing that almost 45 per cent of males had fathers in traditional working-class occupations, and yet only 3 per cent are employed in such occupations. Social mobility from the working class has occurred through both credentialism (30 per cent) and increased opportunities for new forms of managerial and technical activity within the service industries (65 per cent). Of those with social origins in the traditional middle class, 40 per cent of the sample, 40 per cent of these are employed as professionals and 49 per cent as managers.

The income distributions between professionals and managers show that only 35 per cent of professionals are located in the highest income categories, compared with 56 per cent of managers, findings which may be related to gender inequalities, income differentials between parts of the private and public sector, and a decline in economic reward for certain types of educational credentialism. As we have already noted, 22 per cent of females are employed as professionals, compared with only 5 per cent who are employed as managers. Public sector professionals such as teachers and social workers are relatively poorly paid given their levels of educational capital.

With regard to the relationship between education, social origin and occupation while 70 per cent of professionals are graduates, this applies to only 36 per cent of managers. Relating this to the finding that the highest levels of educational qualification are obtained by 40 per cent of those from working-class back-grounds and almost 50 per cent of those from middle-class backgrounds (Table 4.8) leads to the suggestion that any cultural cleavage within the new middle class may relate more to educational level and its corresponding effects upon occupational choice than to initial class of origin.

Given the divisions apparent with regard to the type of occupational activity undertaken according to educational level, the gendered nature of the occupational structure and the changed relationship in the occupational structure between those of differing social origins, it may well be that we can identify forms of cleavage within the new middle class which together may produce important variations in social practice with regard to leisure and other non-work activities. The suggestion is that it is educational and other forms of capital, in combination with occupational activity, that differentiate within the new middle class. It is these differing combinations that may produce the cultural cleavage referred to by Goldthorpe (1987).

Although those subjects with an upward social trajectory share a habitus formed in the past through working-class culture, the formation of the habitus since leaving the parental home has been very different for those whose social positions have been obtained through the accumulation of educational capital. For these subjects the links to their roots have been stretched not only in time and geographical space but most importantly in social space. The spatial features of graduate education are significant, particularly in the UK where it is common for undergraduates to leave the parental home on beginning their studies. Indeed, the spatial relocation associated with 'going to college' has become an important 'rite de passage', particularly for the children of parents in low socio-economic groups. It is during these college years, where new friendships are made and new 'homes' created, that those of lower socio-economic origin begin their movement in both physical and social space away from their parents. This is not to suggest that they are welcomed into higher socio-economic groupings but rather that what was once perhaps most meaning-ful to them in viewing a future life course becomes less so as potential alternatives emerge. The maxim that 'education broad-ens the horizons' is nowhere more true than here – where it has been used quite literally to accomplish this feat. By contrast, those whose current positions did not require the same degree of movement in physical space, at least at the crucial time of late adolescence and early adult life, may have retained an identity associated with that of their forebears, even though the conditions under which it is expressed are considerably more materially comfortable. Even here the marks of their travel through social space will have been made upon the habitus.

Using Bourdieu's terminology, this educational experience forms a part of the habitus that allows the individual to make a different sense of work and to locate it in a frame of reference that is fundamentally different to that employed by those who have not had such an experience. In short, such differences as we have observed may be associated with important cultural variations that give rise to 'a struggle in the social space' of the new middle classes which can be evidenced in other arenas of their everyday lives.

5

THE SOCIAL SPACE OF
LIFESTYLES

In the previous chapter we uncovered some important differences within our sample related to social origin and education and we related these to other contemporary research on the new middle class. It appeared that the differences that were uncovered related also to occupational activities, particularly the distinctions between professionals and managers. In order to make sense of these distinctions we used Bourdieu's conception of the habitus, economic and cultural capital.

In this chapter we will look at friendship patterns and social networks and with some of the leisure and sports practices of residents of The Heath. Of particular interest will be the analysis of the use made of The Heath's clubhouse and associated recreational facilities, which are seen by many residents of The Heath, and some of those in the village, as an important defining characteristic of the estate and its residents. Conversations with residents reveal that these facilities are for some the principal reason for living on The Heath, and they make extensive use of them. For others the appeal of The Heath is more the exclusivity associated with both the private nature of the recreational facilities and the physically bounded nature of the estate itself than the use they make of the available facilities.

Apart from two entrances to the estate from two small country roads, The Heath is surrounded by 'green belt' farming land. Once 'on' The Heath one has entered a private housing estate whose 'gatekeepers' – the residents themselves – in addition to the clubhouse steward that they employ, perform their neighbourhood 'watching' with varying degrees of vigilance. Following both Bourdieu (1984) and more recent contemporary commentators on changing lifestyles (Featherstone, 1991; Rojek,

1994 and 1995) it will be argued that the use of The Heath's recreational facilities and the way that they are organised by residents, provide a crucial indicator of what we can term 'the social space of lifestyles' (Wynne, 1990). Furthermore, the differential use of these facilities and their management helps to provide us with an understanding of what Bourdieu has termed the 'struggle for legitimation in social practice' (Bourdieu, 1977).

The developing tenet of our argument is that the new middle class or service class is not a homogenous social grouping and that this lack of homogeneity can be evidenced at the cultural level. Related to this it is also argued that non-work practices are becoming an increasingly salient feature of this new middle class(es).This is not to suggest that work itself has become unimportant for this social grouping(s) but rather that the role it plays in the construction of identity cannot be assumed to be as salient for the new middle class as it is or was for both the traditional middle and working classes. Whereas it can be supposed from an earlier community studies tradition that the nature of work forms the basis for all other types of sociability (Dennis *et al.*, 1969) and that relations to the means of production are the essential determining features, it is suggested here that relations to the means of consumption are becoming an increasingly important defining characteristic of new social groupings. While it is recognised that such an argument is primarily epistemological rather than empirical, the primary concern here is to provide some empirical indicators to support the contention. We can examine this possibility by an analysis of the patterns of sociability of the sample and their recreational and leisure practices, particularly their use of the recreational facilities at the residents' clubhouse.

The analysis begins with an examination of the frequency distributions discovered in the responses to the questionnaire. The interview data is used to show in more detail the ways in which the statistical findings can be understood as a general representation of the everyday practices of residents. It is suggested that there are indeed distinctions to be drawn, particularly with regard to some of the findings presented in the previous chapter, and that these play a significant role in understanding the heterogeneity of the new middle classes. With regard to the empirical site of this study it is suggested that it reveals a contestation in the construction of the everyday lives of residents which can be seen in their leisure practices and understood with regard to their social origins, educational background and occupations. Following Bourdieu, it is argued that these factors are best understood as together forming that part of the habitus – a structured structure – that acts as a structuring structure in everyday life. The contests referred to can be witnessed in the way in which accepted social practices associated with the use of the recreational facilities are produced, particularly in the definitions of each other developed by the residents themselves. We are not suggesting that these socially constructed categories are mutually exclusive, nor do we claim that such distinctions can be observed in sites other than the one we have examined. However, we would contend that similar 'practices of distinction' will be produced elsewhere amongst the new middle classes and that the indicators identified are perhaps the most salient features associated with these 'cultural' distinctions. Before developing this theme further it is necessary to examine the data collected. Among the indicators examined in this study are those relating to friendship patterns, club and voluntary association membership, sports and wider leisure activities.

FRIENDSHIP PATTERNS

The study reveals that very few residents visit work colleagues and few claim friendships with those living in the nearby villages, despite the fact that it is there that the nearest shops, local library, primary and junior schools are located. Similarly, three nearby churches, two Anglican and one Methodist, are located in these villages. Corresponding social activities and voluntary associations also exist in the local villages and these range from clubs for children such as Cubs, Brownies, Guides and Scouts, to other 'adult' associations connected to the schools, churches, library and pubs. Very few of The Heath's residents either contribute to or make use of these facilities. Indeed, conversations with the local junior school headmaster reveal that The Heath's residents are seen as making virtually no contribution to the life of the school in terms of membership of parent-teacher associations or as school helpers at fund-raising events. A similar pattern emerged from conversations with the local librarian and the Chair of the Playing Fields' Association – neither could remember more than one or two visitors to the 'hobby/interest' clubs that take place in the evenings and afternoons at the library (librarian) or membership of any of the sports clubs that use the village playing fields.

An indication of the relationship of The Heath to at least some of those living in the village is evidenced in the differing approaches taken to a charitable, 'It's A Knockout!' competition. The Playing Fields Association advertised the event some months in advance as part of its centennial celebrations. The formation of local teams was encouraged and various groups entered the competition including the village football team, two teams drawn from local pubs, a team of primary and junior schoolteachers and teams formed from groups of neighbours in the village. The team that entered from The Heath had received a written invitation to do so from the Chair of the Playing Fields Association. The letter had been addressed to the clubhouse manager who had passed it to the squash first team captain. For three weeks prior to the event trials were organised on The Heath for prospective participants and events similar to those planned on the day were run, with the winners making up The Heath's team. Needless to say, on the day of the competition itself The Heath's team was the overwhelming winner, coming first in all but one of nine events. At one period of the competition I overhead a villager shouting at the top of his voice, 'come on, come on, come on, anybody . . . as long as it's not the bloody Heath again!'

On The Heath friendships are associated primarily with other residents of the estate, or with friends made in previous residential locations rather than through integration into the village. Neighbourliness, as opposed to friendships, however, does not appear to be a particularly prominent feature of The Heath with fewer than 20 per cent of households expressing an intimate relationship with their neighbours. It would appear that the friendships made on The Heath are made through the social construction of communities of interest, rather than from necessity, echoing previous differences observed between working- and middle-class friendship patterns rather than any privatisation thesis (Devine, 1992b). It is not so much that residents of The Heath are privatised but that their friendship choices depend less on any necessity for 'good relations with neighbours' and more on a choice of 'who to mix with' according to criteria of interest relating to leisure preferences. In conducting the interviews it became clear that friendships related far more to such leisure

72

preferences, including the use made of the clubhouse and membership of various 'activity associations'.

> We moved here four years ago, just before Becky was born and after Jim had become distribution director. Well, you know . . . the best estate around here, the houses are well built and different, and the club . . . convenient, safe, pleasant surroundings, nice type of people, just, well . . . good. Neighbours, we know them but that's not the point, we don't mix in the sense of spending time with them, they're there but we're not close, most of our friends are people we've met in the bar, a good lot, we have a lot of fun.
>
> It just seems the right place to be. We did well over the previous few years and were living in Middlewich before we moved here. A reward really, for a lot of hard work . . . running a business. We knew of this place from some friends who live here and we wanted to move here for a while – we've had a lot of good times with friends here – smashing. The idea's a good one [clubhouse] and there's no riff-raff – the prices see to that . . . well it is not cheap is it? . . . and there's the annual fee . . . but it's a good idea. SNOB !

For the many households with children, they also become an important part of the 'friend-making' process.

> I suppose most of my friends have been made either through the tennis or the car run. Our closest friends both play tennis and that means we see them a lot playing, have barbecues together in the summer, go to the same dinner parties, and occasionally go to things off The Heath such as the theatre . . . The car run involves taking the children to school and picking them up. One of us will do the morning run and someone else the afternoon. There are five of us involved altogether and it means that we don't have the strain of doing it all the time. Once they're gone in the morning I've got the rest of the day to myself for cleaning and shopping, cooking or whatever. Sometimes, well quite often really – I think it was everyday last week – X came round with Y after dropping the children at school and we drank coffee and chatted for an hour or so.

... [we talk] about lots of things, how the children are doing, if we are going anywhere [out for the evening], tennis, women's things . . . ooh, I don't know. Last week X and I asked Y if she and [husband] were interested in coming to France with us in June. We're going to the Dordogne again, can't wait . . . well look at the weather. We'll stay in the same place as before, a *gîte* rented from 'interhome'. It's just a holiday company really, but I think it began as an owners thing, renting out cottages that they owned – but they got bigger and now I think some of the places are owned by companies rather than individuals as before. The travel is the worst, last year the children were awful but once we're there its wonderful. Walking, eating, drinking, sleeping – and the sun! I take lots of books and read about ten novels in three weeks. I ran out last year and bought two in France, in English of course!

One interesting feature to come from these conversations was the way in which these women, home-based and not in full-time employment, saw the 'car run' and looking after their children and the home as an alternative to full-time employment, which for them had been given up immediately prior to the birth of their first children.

I think all of us worked originally. I was a civil servant working for the DHSS until Emily was born. I supposed I enjoyed it . . . work and the money was handy then, X hasn't always been . . .

When asked the location of their current friends (Figure 5.1) relatively few respondents indicated that their friends were the people that they worked with (15 per cent). That most indicated that their friends came from 'elsewhere' (43 per cent) is perhaps primarily indicative of the fact that many of the respondents had lived on The Heath for a relatively short period of time. Even so The Heath remained the next most popular location category for 'friends' (36 per cent), suggesting that geographical proximity, when coupled with social proximity, remains an important indicator of friendship patterns. The local village accounted for few of the friends of The Heath's residents (8 per cent), which is almost certainly related to the fact that in the immediate area residents of The Heath were invariably seen as people who thought themselves 'better than' the local population, although many of the

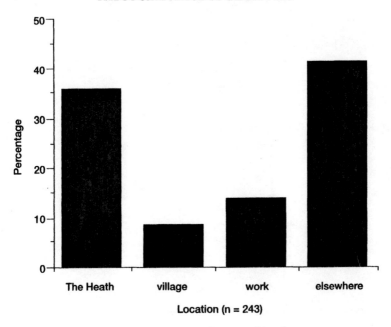

Figure 5.1 Location of current friends

residents of this dormitory village were employed in similar occupations themselves. Almost certainly the physical distance of The Heath from the village, and the 'self-servicing' of leisure activities provided by The Heath's 'clubhouse' amenities are major factors influencing the results obtained.

A further indication of the nature of the friendship patterns enjoyed is the frequency of visits to friends in different locations (Figure 5.2). Almost 60 per cent of respondents rarely visited work colleagues, and less than 10 per cent indicated that they visited such colleagues often. The most frequent visits to friends were either with friends made from previous residential locations (32 per cent) or with friends from The Heath itself (22 per cent).

Figure 5.3 provides an indication of one of the types of sociability particularly popular amongst residents of The Heath, namely the 'dinner' or 'dinner party' – inviting friends around for a drink and meal at the weekends. Almost 50 per cent of households engaged in this form of home entertaining at least once every six weeks. When one takes account of the custom and practice of reciprocity and notes that, on The Heath at least, such dinner

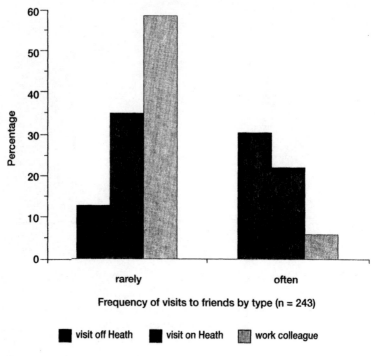

Figure 5.2 Visiting friends

parties usually comprise between four and eight guests, one can see that the dinner party formed an important part of the nature of sociability for many of The Heath's residents. Indeed, obtaining or not obtaining regular and frequent invitations to dinner parties is a particularly salient feature of life on The Heath for many, a feature that is further supported in Figure 5.3, where 'the party' is clearly the most popular form of the leisure activities reported.

> Going out? Well it depends what you mean . . . with the children at this stage we tend to stay on The Heath, rather than go out, but . . . oh yes we have regular dates, and they come round here. I suppose we are somewhere most weekends, in fact we've been somewhere every weekend for as long as, at least the past five weeks, and on the 25th [two weeks' time] we're having them round here.

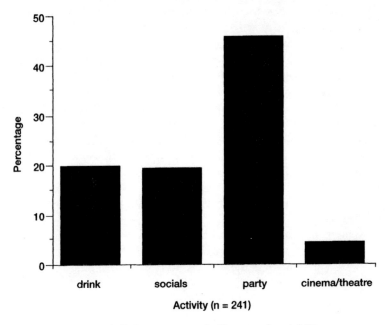

Figure 5.3 Going out: some indicators of sociability

Sometimes we have parties where each couple brings a course, we all contribute to the meal, you know, starters, main course, dessert, cheese and the drinks. Its good because it doesn't put all that pressure on one person. Cooking a meal for eight people can be very fraught so doing it like this makes it easier, and more friendly, less formal, less of a show.

THE CLUBHOUSE

A distinguishing feature of The Heath as a residential estate is the existence of the recreational and leisure facilities available to residents. Such facilities, although unusual when this estate was first built, are becoming increasingly common. They can perhaps be seen as part of the increasing commodification of leisure facilities and part of a self-servicing economy (Pahl, 1984). In an interview for this study the managing director of the company responsible for the development of this estate suggested that people were increasingly looking for the provision of facilities such as these, particularly in areas such as that in which The Heath is located – predominantly rural with few local facilities for residents. The clubhouse, built in the centre of the estate on the 'village green', houses a licensed 'lounge bar' with a capacity for approximately 150 people, a small adjacent room containing a 'pool table' and a hall or meeting room which is also used to increase the size of the bar for social events. The clubhouse overlooks the 'village green' to the side of which is a patio or outside seating area. A small car park separates the clubhouse from the 'youth club', a building initially used by the developers as a sales office, which was extended and given to residents as the development was completed. Figure 5.4 indicates the frequency of attendance at the clubhouse bar and at the social events that take place in the Clubhouse.

Gender differentiation is an important factor in the social practices associated with drinking in pubs and clubs (Griffen, 1987). Although not shown in these data, but certainly apparent from the

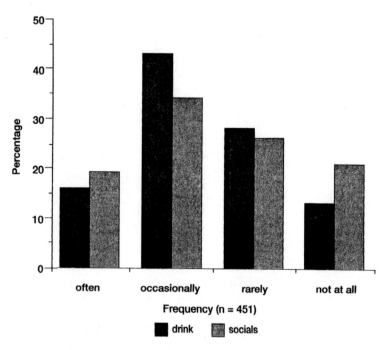

Figure 5.4 The clubhouse and social events

observational work and interviews, the majority of females are invariably accompanied by men when they attend the clubhouse bar. Here we can note that less than 15 per cent of respondents do not use the lounge bar for drinking, 16 per cent drink there often and almost 45 per cent describe themselves as occasional drinkers at the lounge bar.

The figure also provides an indication of attendance at the variety of social events held in the clubhouse bar. The social events are primarily related to seasonal festive occasions and fund-raising activities for the clubs and associations set up by residents. Amongst these are Christmas, New Year, and Valentine's Day dances, an annual Summer Barbecue, a bonfire and fireworks display in November on Guy Fawkes night, and a number of fund-raising discos for clubs and associations. The frequency distributions are very similar to those for drinking. Only 20 per cent of respondents do not attend social events at all, 19 per cent attend often and 34 per cent describe themselves as 'occasional' attenders. More than anything else, these figures appear to suggest some differentiation between those who make use of the facilities and those who do not. Like those 'often' and 'occasional' drinkers (59 per cent), 'often' and 'occasional' attendees at social events (53 per cent) comprise over 50 per cent of the respondents. At the same time there is a substantial proportion of 'non and rare users' of these facilities.

Further data that provide some indicators of the styles of life of the sample concerns possession of a variety of consumer durables associated with leisure activities and other pastimes. These include ownership of three television sets or more (20 per cent), two cars or more (74 per cent), video recorders (60 per cent) and computers (38 per cent), and expenditure on major items of leisure equipment such as boats, caravans and second homes (22 per cent). Clearly the residents of The Heath enjoy an affluent lifestyle with considerable expenditure on consumer durables and leisure goods.

In addition to the lounge bar, pool room and meeting room the clubhouse contains two squash courts, an indoor heated swimming pool, a sauna and changing rooms. The recreational facilities also include two hard floodlit tennis courts. Figure 5.5 provides an overview of the frequency of use of these sports facilities.

Swimming is by far the most popular activity, defined in terms of the frequency of participation and of the numbers of participants.

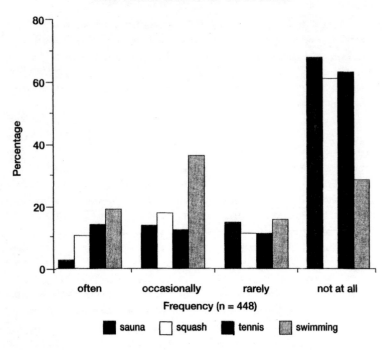

Figure 5.5 Use of clubhouse recreational facilities

Almost 20 per cent of respondents are frequent users of this facility and over 35 per cent classify themselves as occasional users. Fewer than 30 per cent say that they do not use the facility at all. In contrast very few respondents, less than 3 per cent, use the sauna frequently and almost 70 per cent of respondents say that they do not use the sauna at all. With respect to the two racket sports, tennis and squash, we can note that just over 10 per cent say that they play squash often and 14 per cent play tennis often. A further 19 per cent (squash) and 12 per cent (tennis) describe themselves as 'occasional' users. In short, both the tennis and squash facilities appear to be popular for a significant number of residents.

To understand further how these sports facilities are used, together with attitudes to sports and the sports facilities on The Heath, it is necessary to consider previous sports activity. Figure 5.6 provides some indication by examining participation in sports at school.

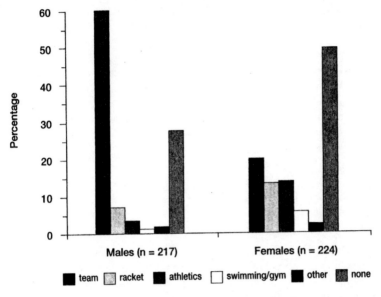

Figure 5.6 Sports participation at school

Team games were the predominant form of school sports activity
for both males and females, although it should be noted that three
times as many males (60 per cent) participated in team sports as
females (20 per cent). It is also worth noting that fewer males (27
per cent) than females (50 per cent) did not participate in sport at
school, other than compulsory physical education. Although the
other sports that appear tend to have higher participation rates
amongst females than among males this might be explained by
the fact that schools, especially state schools, have tended traditionally to concentrate upon team activities, football, cricket,
hockey, rugby, netball as compared to non-team sports. Consequently, given the much higher participation rates in team
sports by males over females, it is perhaps not surprising that
females appear to engage in these other sports more frequently
than males. At the same time it should be remembered that racket
sports, the principal school sport being tennis, require considerable investment in terms of time and coaching in order for an
individual to become reasonably proficient, and again it is perhaps no surprise that such sports do not figure particularly highly
amongst this population, approximately 45 per cent of whom

come from working-class backgrounds. Consequently, although sports activity at school was relatively popular, it is not surprising that most respondents did not play racket sports whilst at school.

Sports, well not really, not at school apart from PT and games. But when we arrived here it seemed that all the people we were introduced to either played squash or tennis so we joined in . . . well squash, not tennis . . . that's more for the experts, but with squash its not so difficult; you can have a good game even if you're not good yourself by playing with people of the same standard. That's why the leagues are so good. You get at least six games a month plus others, and it keeps you fit. In the leagues I go up and down, up and down all the time, but I really enjoy it and I've, we've, made a lot of very good friends through the squash.

I'd played some tennis at school, I suppose a lot really, yes it was wonderful, long sunny days, tennis yes and lots of school friends; really halcyon days, just like *Schoolfriend*! Not so much at university, not at all. I thought I'd left it behind until we moved here. Now it's become a large part of my life again, along with the golf. I suppose it is difficult to learn, but I haven't really noticed that . . . when you're young you learn without any effort really, like riding a bicycle.

Thursday is squash night, league night. At the moment I'm in the second team, and that's largely due to position in the internal leagues – the squash ladder that we have here. Well there are some players, one or two, who don't play all their internal games, but are so good that they play in the first team, well one is with us now in the second team. Anyhow, if I can just hold it a bit more, a bit longer I'll be in the firsts soon – right now that's what I'm aiming for. I've played for them once or twice but I really want a regular place. It's very competitive but so it should be, what's the use of playing if it isn't?

Waste of good drinking time . . . we're waiting for the first heart attack anyhow, bloody fools, and they think they're so good. We don't have that much to do with them. Some of them will have a drink in here but a lot you never see, they just go straight home. Well he's (. . .) different, he does play but not like they do, he enjoys it, for a bit of exercise, something to do, then he's in here with us.

less competitive.

For the most part social origin, measured by father's occupational position (Figure 5.7), does not appear to have a significant effect on the most frequent sports players, other than those from the lowest socio-economic backgrounds. Those from occupational category 4 only appear amongst the more frequent users of the swimming pool where approximately 18 per cent of them 'frequently' engage in this activity. This compares with 24 per cent in category 1, 11 per cent in category 2 and 21 per cent in category 3.

Use of the sauna is very much a minority activity for all, irrespective of social background. Approximately 18 per cent of those from category 1 are frequent squash players, 14 per cent from category 2 and 25 per cent from category 3. Tennis is a frequent activity for approximately 13 per cent of those in category 1, 12 per cent in category 2 and 17 per cent in category 3.

However, when controls are introduced for 'educational capital' a quite different picture emerges (Figure 5.8). Here we

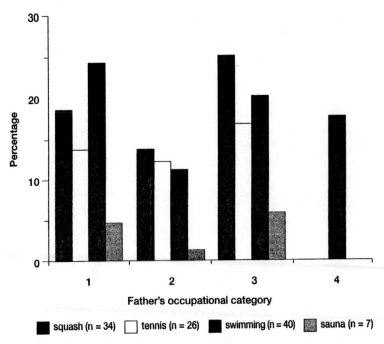

Figure 5.7 Social origin and sport (males): per cent from father's occupational categories selecting 'often'

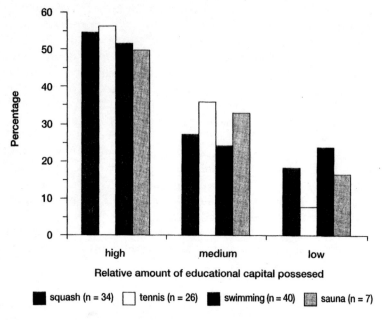

Figure 5.8 Participation in clubhouse sports by educational level (males): respondents answering 'often'

can clearly see the effects of such capital with regard to the most 'frequent users' of the recreational facilities. The higher the educational capital, the greater the likelihood of 'frequent' participation. In each of the four recreational practices over 50 per cent of the most frequent users can be found to possess high amounts of such capital. Those with low amounts of educational capital are less likely to be frequent users of the recreational facilities. Approximately 17 per cent of the most frequent squash players have low amounts of educational capital, 7 per cent of the tennis players, 24 per cent of swimmers and 17 per cent of the sauna users.

LEISURE, LIFESTYLE AND THE HABITUS

It was suggested in the previous chapter that the population of The Heath can best be described as belonging to a new middle class which has emerged from the occupational changes associated with an increasing credentialism and, importantly, from the emergence of an increased managerialism in a changing economy which has outstripped the supply of graduate labour to the work force. Our examination and analysis of the social characteristics of residents of The Heath suggested that rather than being an homogenous social grouping, there were rather significant differences in types of occupational activity which corresponded to differences in both social origin and educational level. By employing Bourdieu's concepts of capital and the habitus it has been argued that the differences observed are such that we can distinguish between those employed in professional occupations and those in management occupations with regard to their social origins, education, income and gender. The following picture emerged:

1 Mobility for males of working-class origin had come about primarily through occupational advancement and promotion (65 per cent), rather than through educational advancement into professional activity.
2 Almost half of the women in our sample defined themselves as housewives. Occupational activity for the highest educationally qualified females was primarily as professionals, with only 5 per cent employed as managers.
3 Those with origins in the traditional middle class were more evenly spread between professional employment (40 per cent) and managerial employment (49 per cent).
4 Income differentials between professionals and managers were such that managers more than professionals were most likely to be found in the highest income category (56 per cent cf. 36 per cent).
5 Those with the highest educational levels were better represented in the professional category (70 per cent) than in the management category (36 per cent).

Thus it was argued that the new middle class, rather than being a relatively homogenous class fraction, might display characteristics of cultural cleavage as suggested in Goldthorpe's *Social Mobility and Class Structure in Modern Britain* (1987).

Tables 5.1–5.3 provide a series of indicators with regard to social networks and the leisure and sports activities associated with the use of the clubhouse. These indicators are examined according to the 'structured habitus' of respondents produced from our investigations in Chapter 4. Table 5.1 examines the friendship patterns of The Heath's residents. Together with the interview materials and the ethnographic data that are presented in Chapter 7, the table helps to construct a picture of the nature of these friendships and their relationship to social origin and educational capital. The figures do suggest some differences according to educational capital possessed and indicate that those with the least amounts of such capital (managerial and other non-professional occupations) are more likely to construct friendships around residential location (columns 2 and 3) and associated 'neighbourliness' (columns 5 and 6) than are those with the highest levels of educational capital (university graduates and professional occupations). For those with low educational capital friendships tend to be made with others 'on The Heath' and at previous residential locations, while for those of working-class origin with the highest amounts of educational capital friendship patterns are more than three times as likely to be associated with work colleagues (18 per cent cf. 5 per cent, column 4).

Table 5.2 is constructed from a series of indicators associated with the use of The Heath's clubhouse other than for sports activities. In this table the primary concern is to establish the use of the clubhouse for social activities such as parties (the Summer Barbecue and Christmas Dance) and the more casual 'going for a drink' at the clubhouse bar.

Again, it can be seen that it is those with the least amounts of educational capital who are the most frequent users of the non-sports facilities at the clubhouse, with those of working-class origin being particularly prominent in attending and organising the social calendar and using the clubhouse to 'go for a drink', while the most highly educated of those with middle-class origins are the least likely participants in these activities.

Table 5.3 examines the sports histories and current sports practices of residents with regard to their social origins and educational level. The table shows the frequency results from a series of questions relating to sports activities at school, new sports taken up since leaving school, current membership of sports clubs other than on The Heath and finally, the use of sports facilities provided on The Heath. Each of these factors is examined according to the social origin and educational level of the respondent. The figures are suggestive of a link between social origin/educational capital and sports histories and the use of the

Table 5.1 The habitus and lifestyle indicators (percentage) (n = 185)

Social origin and ed. capital	Visit friends 'off' The Heath	Visit friends 'on' The Heath	Visit work colleagues	Majority of friends on The Heath	Know neighbour 'well'	'Entertain' at home (every 6 weeks)	Attend parties on The Heath (every 12 weeks)
All	30	19	8	36	16	47	35
w/c high ed. (n=32)	22	11	18	18	15	17	20
m/c high ed. (n=50)	15	5	5	21	13	31	25
w/c low ed. (n=49)	48	30	5	27	35	26	37
m/c low ed. (n=54)	35	30	5	34	32	26	18

Notes: w/c = working class
m/c = middle class

Table 5.2 The habitus and the clubhouse (percentage) (n = 185)

Social origin and ed. capital		Attending social activity at club	Organise 'events'	Social event elsewhere with partner	Drink at clubhouse (males)	Drink at clubhouse (females)	Visiting club with partner (often)
All	often	21	14	25	22	14	20
	rarely	47	—	—	36	45	—
w/c high ed. (n=32)	often	22	24	17	22	17	8
m/c high ed. (n=50)	often	11	24	26	20	8	26
w/c low ed. (n=49)	often	38	38	13	33	42	40
m/c low ed. (n=54)	often	30	14	43	25	33	29

Notes: see Table 5.1

Table 5.3 The habitus and sports practices (males) (percentage) (n = 185)

Social origin and ed. capital	Sport at school	School sport type	Sports since school	New sport type	Members of sports clubs	Swim at The Heath female/male	Tennis at The Heath female/male	Squash at The Heath female/male
All	73	63 team 14 racket	60	34 racket 9 golf 8 keep-fit 1 team	20	33/34	29/25	17/30
w/c high ed. (n=32)	73	66 team	66	44 racket 13 golf 6 keep-fit	10	35/40	40/39	26/40
m/c high ed. (n=50)	76	67 team 10 racket	73	40 racket 10 keep-fit 8 golf	29	27/35	23/27	12/36
w/c low ed. (n=49)	69	63 team	53	26 racket 12 keep-fit 12 golf 2 team	14	40/30	23/15	9/20
m/c low ed. (n=54)	72	55 team 15 racket	49	26 racket 11 golf 4 keep-fit	25	27/32	24/19	9/25

Notes: see Table 5.1

recreational facilities provided on The Heath. Clearly the majority of male respondents, irrespective of social origin/educational level (column 1), played sports at school other than compulsory physical education (column 2). The appearance of racket sports in column 3, the type of sports played at school, is less important for its frequency than it is for its presence amongst those with middle-class rather than working-class social origins – its presence indicating that racket sports are primarily associated with children of middle-class rather than working-class parents. Columns 4 and 5 present the data on sports that have been taken up since leaving the school system and show that those who did not enter higher education are less likely to have taken up new sports than those who did enter higher education (column 4). The types of new sports taken up are shown in column 5 and indicate differences in response particularly in regard to racket sports. Although in each category racket sports, golf and keep-fit have been taken up, take-up rates of racket sports are considerably higher for those in the highest educational category for males. The frequency distribution on membership of sports clubs, other than those established on The Heath (column 6), are important in that the figures indicate that it is those of middle-class social origin, rather than those of working-class origin, who are most likely to join 'off Heath' sports clubs. Such figures suggest that those of middle-class origin are less likely to use The Heath's facilities as their sole source of recreational activity. Columns 7, 8 and 9 provide an indication of the use of The Heath's sports facilities amongst the most frequent users, defined as those using these facilities at least twice a month. Although differential use of the swimming pool is not particularly high, differences in the use of the squash and tennis facilities are notable. For males the figures indicate that those with working-class origins who have experienced higher education are twice as likely to play squash or tennis as those with working-class origins who have not experienced higher education, and are more likely to be regular swimmers. Although the differentials are less strong, a similar situation pertains for those males of middle-class backgrounds who have experienced higher education, compared to those who have not. Although the 'direction' of these findings is similar to those for females, it appears that the relationships are less strong (see Chapter 6).

The tentative suggestion from these findings is that non-work practices, particularly those associated with The Heath's club-house facilities, are an important defining characteristic of residents and help form lifestyle distinctions between them. When we recall the data examined in the previous chapter it becomes possible to relate the variables examined there and the differences associated with professional and managerial occupations to the observed differences in the non-work practices of residents indicated in Tables 5.1–5.3.

CONCLUSION

Our data presents a picture suggestive of heterogeneity rather than homogeneity and lends support for our developing central tenet. Alongside the homologies associated with social origin, occupational position, educational and economic capital discovered in the previous chapter, we have found a number of defining characteristics that suggest a cultural heterogeneity within the sample. In addition to differentiation in friendship patterns and social activities which form part of the everyday lives of residents, our analysis has found distinctions in the 'recreational/sports' histories and current 'recreational/sports' practices of the sample. In each of these areas of everyday life differences are observed according to 'structural' backgrounds. For example, although the numbers expressing friendships with work colleagues were generally low, those with social origins in the working class with the highest educational levels were three times more likely to have friendships associated with work colleagues than others (18 per cent cf. 5 per cent). By contrast, while dinner parties were one of the most popular forms of 'entertainment' (47 per cent), their popularity is lowest amongst those with working-class origins and high educational levels (17 per cent). This same group is amongst the most frequent users of the sports facilities on The Heath, although this is not transferred into membership of other sports clubs. Rather such membership is primarily associated with those of middle-class origin (27 per cent cf. 12 per cent). Conversely it is the use of The Heath's clubhouse bar and lounge that is overwhelmingly associated with those of working-class origin and low educational levels (38 per cent).

More generally we can also acknowledge distinctions uncovered in the observational and interview data which, in combination, provide evidence to substantiate those claims that would argue that there is indeed differentiation within the formation of the new middle class. On The Heath it appears that it is those of working-class origin who are the prime users of the recreational facilities, the bar being primarily associated with those who have the lowest educational levels ('drinkers') and the sports with those who have the highest educational levels ('sporters') (Wynne, 1990). The picture presented allows for the construction of what might be termed the social space of lifestyles on The Heath through a model similar to that constructed at the end of the previous chapter. The results of these previous investigations into social origin, occupational position, educational and economic capital have been represented in a model of what we termed 'the social space of mobility' (Figure 4.1). By relating the results of the investigations in this chapter to that model of 'social position' we can construct a second diagram of what could be termed 'the social space of lifestyles' (Figure 5.9). In this diagram the horizontal and vertical axes of economic and educational capital are retained, as are the socio-economic origins of the new middle class(es): both the traditional working and middle classes. Occupational positions are replaced by the lifestyle indicators examined in this chapter. Such a model indicates that the new middle class exhibits a series of lifestyle choices, structured by, and structuring of, its habitus. If this map of lifestyles is placed over our map of social mobility then it can be seen that there are important differences associated with those mobility paths. These differences include the nature of friendship patterns, the use of the recreational facilities available to residents, their sports histories and their current sports participation. By overlaying Figure 4.1 with Figure 5.9 in this way, we can see the developing homologies within the new middle class(es). Together the diagrams illustrate those differences between what one might broadly describe as professional and managerial workers. Such observations have been supported by recent work by Savage et al. (1992:141–144) who, on the basis of research conducted by the British Market Research Bureau involving a Target Group Index analysis of a limited number of consumer items, have also suggested that lifestyle distinctions may be developing between professional and managerial fractions within the middle class.

In order to understand these distinctions more fully it is necessary to examine what de Certeau (1984) has termed the 'practices of use' associated with these discovered differences, i.e. the ways

THE SOCIAL SPACE OF LIFESTYLES

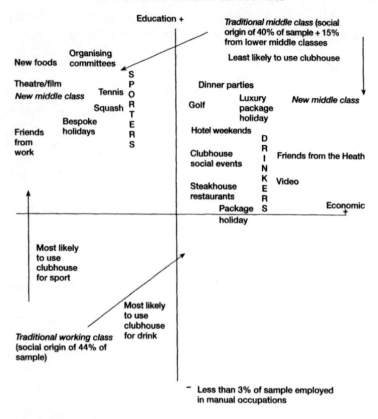

Notes: (i) Although the numbers expressing friendships with work colleagues were low, those with social origins in the working class with high educational levels were three times more likely to have friendships associated with work colleagues than others (18% cf. 5%).

(ii) Dinner parties were one of the most popular forms of 'entertainment', yet were least popular amongst those with working-class origins and high educational levels.

(iii) The use of the clubhouse bar (non-sports facilities) was overwhelmingly associated with those of working-class origin and low educational levels (38% cf. 11% of middle-class origin with high educational level).
Only 8% of women with middle-class origins and of high educational level attended the clubhouse, compared with 40% of women of working-class origin and low educational levels.

(iv) Squash and tennis were primarily associated with those of working-class origin and high educational levels (39% tennis and 40% squash compared with 15% and 20% of those of working-class origin and low educational levels).

(v) Membership of sports clubs (golf?) not on The Heath was primarily associated with those of middle-class origin (27% cf. 12%).

Figure 5.9 The social space of leisure

92

in which everyday life is constructed and maintained through the activities of individuals and social groups such that particular activities come to be understood as having a particular nature or organisational form. What this examination requires is ethnographic material that attends to the ways in which these differences emerge and are maintained to produce the differing habit-uses associated with these class fractions. Such an analysis needs to uncover the ways in which 'going for a drink' or 'playing tennis or squash' are accomplished, such that they become defining characteristics of those who participate in and organise such activities. To that end Chapter 7 examines the ways in which the clubhouse and recreational facilities are used and organised, and the ways in which such use is responded to by others.

6

THE SOCIAL SPACE OF GENDER

We have argued in earlier chapters that the new middle class cannot be understood as a homogenous social group. Rather, we have outlined a series of 'boundaries' associated with social origin, education and occupation which can be seen to relate to the interests, tastes and leisure preferences of particular social groups. Of course, such findings need to be examined in the context of the households through which our subjects' lives are lived. To that end this chapter examines the structure of the households on The Heath with regard to our thesis of fragmentation and the relationship between gender differentiation, domestic labour and leisure.

The Heath is a place for nuclear families; a place for new families to plan children, and for families with children. It is not a place for young single people or single parent families. Data from the questionnaire reveal that only 29 households (11.6 per cent) are single households. Clearly a number of factors mitigate against such household formation. First, the houses themselves are designed for families, with two, three or four bedrooms, 'working' kitchens and 'utility' rooms. Second, the pricing structure of the properties also places them out of the reach of all but the most wealthy of single, young people. Third, its location in the countryside green belt and the ambiance associated with the development make The Heath unattractive to young, single persons.

Nor is The Heath a place, as yet, for the retired. At first glance The Heath may appear attractive to the elderly but on closer inspection there is perhaps less appeal. The absence of everyday facilities such as local shops and ancillary services are factors which might discourage the elderly from moving on to The

Heath, although for those who are still relatively mobile, in good health and only recently retired, it does offer some of the facilities associated with 'retirement communities' similar to those that have recently appeared in the USA.

However, for the most part The Heath is dominated by nuclear families with relatively young, school age children. Certainly it is for such people that The Heath was built and to whom it is marketed – as a place where the family can retreat from the pressures of everyday urban living, where children can play in safety and where the family can offer succour and support for those who ensure its financial provisioning. This is why The Heath was built and this, in large part, is who it attracts. As such The Heath provides an excellent opportunity to examine the structure of the new middle-class household and the extent to which gender differentiation is becoming less salient in understanding this part of everyday life. Indeed, given the importance of the new middle class as an indicator of the changing nature of contemporary British society (Featherstone, 1987 and 1991), it is perhaps on The Heath, as much as anywhere, that we might witness examples of the changing nature of household structures and gender relations. In this chapter we will consider such changes in the context of the analyses previously undertaken, namely their location within the new middle class and the differentiation already observed with regard to educational level, social background and occupation. In examining the relationship between leisure practices and the social construction of identity we have suggested that for the new middle class work is becoming a less salient feature in identity construction and that as working conditions and income become increasingly less differentiated within the new middle class or 'middle mass' (Roberts *et al.*, 1977), so leisure practices will become increasingly important. This, of course, begs a serious question for that part of the new middle class whose relationship to paid work can at best be defined as problematic. Here, of course, I am referring to women, the majority of whom, in the middle classes, have traditionally acted as an unpaid domestic work force, primarily involved in the reproduction of the middle-class household.

Thus this chapter will pay particular attention to gender divisions, household structure and domestic labour and the ways in which these mitigate the differences in leisure lifestyles between males and females. In doing this we will examine the ways in

95

which paid employment affects women's leisure, a feature that Deem suggests may be important in 'allowing' women the right to a leisure space. Commenting on her own study of women's leisure practices and the relationship between leisure and employment she writes,

> What does seem to emerge is that female employment may be as important in structuring women's experience of leisure as male employment is in organising and determining men's leisure. Women in employment frequently, although not always, have greater control and autonomy over their own lives and hence greater control over their leisure, than women who are not in employment.
>
> (Deem, 1986:116)

In addition to examining women's use of the clubhouse facilities on The Heath we will also examine some of the other activities associated with domestic labour and the creation of 'leisure spaces' by women around this domestic labour. Examples of such leisure spaces are associated with child-rearing, 'coffee breaks' and membership of voluntary associations. As both Deem and Green *et al.* (1987), have indicated, many women who are not involved in work outside the home often construct their own leisure spaces in and alongside the routines of domestic labour. Deem makes the point in her discussion of definitional problems,

> Whilst the problems of defining women's leisure are immense anyway, home-based leisure is if anything harder to determine than out-of-home leisure, since it is even more likely to overlap with, or occur concurrently with non-leisure activities.
>
> (Deem, 1986:34)

In similar vein Green *et al.*, in reviewing their own earlier research, comment,

> The leisure activities which women do most frequently and on which they spend the majority of their free time are those that can be done at home; that can be done in the bits of time left over from doing other things, or that can be easily interrupted if necessary.
>
> (Green *et al.*, 1990:84)

As such, Deem argues,

> Women's home-based leisure and enjoyment is often based on or derives from, the same activities and tasks which form part of their work in the household . . . No wonder then that much of women's household leisure consists of needlework, knitting, cooking, reading, TV watching . . . All of these activities can be fitted into a fragmented time schedule, don't require large blocks of time . . . and can be quickly disposed of or stopped when work obligations intervene.
>
> (Deem, 1986:81)

We will also discuss the degree to which men contribute to this everyday domestic labour. While the conjugal role thesis (Parsons, 1952; Goode, 1970; Young and Wilmott, 1960) has received increasing criticism (Oakley, 1974; Edgell, 1980), there is, nevertheless, some confusion over male participation in domestic labour. As Brannen and Moss (1991) indicate,

> A few British studies (Newson and Newson, 1963; Oakley, 1974; Graham and Mckee, 1979) have reported that men in higher status occupations generally do more childcare and domestic work. Other studies, in Britain and elsewhere (for example, Richards *et al.*, 1977; Entwistle and Doering, 1980; Beail, 1983; Russell, 1983; Moss, Bolland and Foxman, 1987) report no difference.
>
> (Brannen and Moss, 1991:182)

However as Green *et al.* point out in commenting upon the differences observed by Sharpe (1984) in comparison with the earlier community studies of Slater and Woodside (1951) and Dennis, Henriques and Slaughter (1969),

> Certainly, significant changes have taken place over the last thirty years in norms about male participation and childcare, and in terms of the tasks which husbands and fathers now do.
>
> (Green *et al.*, 1990:92)

Although we will examine differences in the contributions to domestic labour made by men and women, this chapter will be primarily concerned with locating 'gender' within the model previously outlined, pointing towards social and cultural differentiation within the new middle class and the increasing importance of leisure in the construction of identity. As such our concern will be to uncover any differences with regard to the social origins, educational levels and occupational positions of our subjects.

First we provide a brief outline of the structure of the domestic household obtained from an analysis of the questionnaire.

GENDER DIFFERENTIATION AND THE DOMESTIC HOUSEHOLD

As we saw earlier there are some notable differences in the structural characteristics between males and females, particularly with regard to occupation (Table 3.1), income (Table 3.2) and education (Table 3.3). While over 40 per cent of males are employed as managers, and over 30 per cent as professionals, only 5 per cent (managers) and 22 per cent (professionals) of women are employed in these categories; a further 16 per cent are employed in lower level white collar work including clerical/administrative and sales. Approximately 45 per cent of women described themselves as housewives. Such results are reflected in the income differentials between males and females. Only 5 per cent of women earn more than £15,000 per year compared with 70 per cent of males, and 77 per cent of women earned less than £10,000 per year, compared with only 11 per cent of males. While the number of 'housewives' in the sample clearly affects these figures, they do not solely explain the income differentials between males and females, for example those between male and female professionals are almost certainly related to the types of profession in which females are predominantly found – lower grade salaried professionals in, for example, junior and primary school teaching, social work and other local authority and public services. Differences in educational qualifications obtained indicate that 54 per cent of females are not educated beyond O level compared with 27 per cent of males and that postgraduate/professional qualifications are obtained by only 3 per cent of females in spite of the fact that a similar percentage of males (29 per cent) and females (27 per cent) obtain undergraduate degrees.

We can now turn to an examination of the household in order to see how the gender differences reviewed above are reflected in its composition and how this composition itself relates to those factors we examined earlier in the context of a new middle class fragmented and differentiated by economic and cultural capital.

In the conclusion to Chapter 4 it was suggested that the structural divisions uncovered identified forms of cleavage or fragmentation within the new middle class such that it could not be considered a homogenous grouping and that, rather, social origin, education and occupation combined to produce differentiation in habitus and social practice. Similarly we will now consider the extent to which these divisions are reflected in the household structures on The Heath and the possible differentially gendered nature of these households.

Table 6.1 shows the relationship between the 'habitus' variable (social origin and educational level) for males and females. The cross-tabulation reveals the links between these variables in the structure of the households on The Heath.

The table shows the importance of both social origin and educational level on the structure of the household. Almost half (48.9 per cent) of women located in category 1, working-class origin and lower educational level have partners with the same social background and educational level. Those women in category 1 with partners from different social backgrounds overwhelmingly have partners with similar educational levels – fewer than 14 per

Table 6.1 The habitus, gender and household structure (percentage)
(men: n = 185; women: n = 179)

Men \ Women	w/c low ed. (n = 49)	w/c high ed. (n = 74)	m/c low ed. (n = 74)	m/c high ed. (n = 28)
w/c low ed. (n = 49)	48.9 ↓ 51.2 →	16.7 ↓ 9.3 →	24.2 ↓ 34.9 →	8.7 ↓ 4.7 →
w/c high ed. (n = 32)	8.9 ↓ 14.8	37.5 33.3	14.5 33.3	21.7 18.5
m/c low ed. (n = 54)	28.9 ↓ 29.5	12.5 6.8	40.3 56.8	13 6.8
m/c high ed. (n = 50)	13.3 ↓ 15	33.3 20	24.2 ↓ 32.5	56.5 32.5

Notes: w/c = working class
m/c = middle class

cent of such women have partners from a higher social background and higher educational level. Other categories in this table reveal a similar story with regard to social origin and educational level. Over 70 per cent of the highest educated women from both working-class and middle-class backgrounds have partners with the same educational levels and few households contain women with men of a lower educational level. Households that are divided with regard to social origin and education appear mostly to involve men and women of working-class origin with high educational levels – the highest educated women of working-class origin with the highest educated men of middle-class origin (33.3 per cent), and the highest educated men of working-class origin with the lower educated women of middle-class origin (33.3 per cent).

Table 6.2 examines the relations between occupation, gender and the household. Although 45 per cent of women classed themselves as housewives and therefore represent the largest single 'occupational' category, the location of other working women shows that almost 60 per cent of professional women have partners in professional occupations (58.1 per cent). Given the extremely small number of women in managerial positions (5 per cent) although the majority are married to men in similar positions, such men are most likely to be partnered by housewives (48.8 per cent), an important defining characteristic of the household, particularly with regard to male performance of domestic labour (see p. 105).

These developing relations between education, occupation, social origin and the household are explored further in Table 6.3 which examines the links between the habitus associated with social origin and education and women's occupations.

As can be seen from the table 85 per cent of those classed as housewives are located in the lowest educational categories – category 1, those with working-class origins (33.8 per cent) and category 3, those with middle-class origins (51.4 per cent). Professional women are overwhelmingly from the highest educational category but are almost equally represented with regard to social origin – category 2 (39.6 per cent) and category 4 (37.5 per cent). Clearly little of reliable worth can be stated with regard to managerial occupations given the very small numbers present. Those women in category 3 are primarily working in clerical/ administrative and sales positions (see Table 3.1).

Table 6.2 Occupation, gender and household structure (percentage) (n = 202)

Men \ Women	Professionals (n = 43)	Managers (n = 9)	Tech./clerical/ sales (n = 74)	Unemployed/ retired (n = 28)	Housewife high ed. (n = 28)
Professionals (n = 64)	58.1 ↓ 39.1 →	33.3 ↓ 4.7 →	20 ↓ 15.6 →		28 ↓ 40.6 →
Managers (n = 86)	32.6 ↓ 16.3	44.4 4.7	52 30.2		45.2 48.8
Tech./clerical/sales (n = 85)	9.3 ↓ 11.4	22.2 5.7	26 37.1		17.2 45.7
Unemployed/retired (n = 17)			2 5.9	100 41.2	9.7 52.9

Table 6.3 The habitus and occupations of women (percentage) (n = 178)

	Professionals (n = 48)	Managers (n = 7)	Tech./clerical/ sales (n = 47)	Unemployed/ retired (n = 2)	Housewife (n = 74)
w/c low ed. (n = 49)	4.1 → 4.2 ↓	6.1 → 42.9 ↓	38.8 → 40.4 ↓		51 → 33.8 ↓
w/c high ed. (n = 28)	67.9 39.6 ↓	3.6 14.3	7.1 4.3		21.4 8.1
m/c low ed. (n = 73)	12.3 18.8 ↓	22.2 5.7	31.5 48.9	1.4 50	52.1 51.4
m/c high ed. (n = 28)	64.3 ↓ 37.5 ↓	3.6 14.3	10.7 6.4	3.6 50	17.9 6.8

Notes: Top row in italics indicates differences within capitals
Bottom row indicates differences between capitals
See also notes to Table 6.1

Due to the structure of the questionnaire and the way in which the data were coded it is impossible to provide precise details of household income. Nevertheless with some re-coding of the income variables for males and females it is possible to provide some indication of household income and the structure of its distribution. Table 6.4 below provides an indication of the income levels of individuals and households.

Some 193 households provided data on income. The table shows that single households accounted for only just over 10 per cent of the households on The Heath, confirming the view that The Heath is essentially a place for families. Of the dual households that make up almost 90 per cent of households on The Heath, 35 per cent were single-earner, dual households, and almost all of these were male. The majority of households, 111 of those responding (57 per cent), were dual-earner households. As can be seen from the briefest examination of these figures, women, irrespective of household structure, are found in the lowest income category, under £10,000 per annum, whereas large numbers of men can be found in the highest income category, with very few in the lowest. The figures clearly suggest that in the majority of households women's incomes are significantly less than men's. This tendency can be seen more clearly in Table 6.5 which shows the relationship between male and female incomes in dual-earner households. The figures show that in these dual-earner households only 7 per cent of women earn more than their

Table 6.4 Household structure and income (percentage) (n = 193)

Household Structure	Income			
	Low	Medium	High	
Single				
male	0 →	60 →	40 →	n = 10
female	46 →	54 →	0 →	n = 11
Dual				
single earners:				
male	3 →	46 →	51 →	n = 59
female	100 →	0 →	0 →	n = 2
dual earners:				
male	14 →	53 →	33 →	n = 111
female	80 →	5 →	5 →	n = 111

Table 6.5 Incomes of males and females in dual-earner households
(n = 111)

Male	Female	Percentage
low	l	11
l	m	3
l	h	1
medium	l	40
m	m	10
m	h	3
high	l	28
h	m	3
h	h	1

male partners. The two largest of the dual-earner household combinations are the 'medium–low income' (male–female), accounting for 40 per cent of dual-earner households and the 'high–low income' (male–female), accounting for 28 per cent of dual-earner households.

We have now examined the principal social indicators of household formation with regard to the developing thesis of fragmentation and cultural diversification within the new middle class. From the data examined it would appear that there is support for this thesis and that differentiation in household structure within the new middle class can be supported. Similar to the analyses previously undertaken it appears that structural distinctions can be drawn between households according to the social origin and educational level of their members. Such variables relate both to the nature of household occupations and the structure and amount of household income.

In short it appears that partners tend to have similar educational and socio-economic backgrounds; those males in professional occupations with partners working outside the home are most likely to have professional partners (39 per cent) whereas males in managerial positions are most likely to have partners working as housewives (49 per cent), or in clerical/ administrative and sales (30 per cent). Household income levels between what one might term 'managerial' and 'professional' households are structured around the distinctions between dual and single income households. In this context only 28 per cent of housewives are in professional households whereas 45 per cent are found in managerial households. While the lowest income earning households will be those single earning households in occupational category 3, technical, administrative, sales (8 per cent), the single earning households in occupational category 2, senior and middle management (21 per cent), will be amongst the highest of income earning households, along with some of the dual professionals (12.4 per cent).

Amongst those factors illustrative of the conjugal role thesis, male contributions to everyday domestic labour surely provide an important indicator. For the conjugal role thesis to have any validity one would expect an increasing de-differentiation in the traditional roles accorded to gender in domestic labour activity. Figures 6.1 and 6.2 illustrate the myth of conjugal roles in the domestic labour arrangements for households on The Heath: households of the new middle class, the supposed carriers of the new lifestyles, which include those most likely to exhibit the traits associated with the perceived breakdown of gender divisions.

Figures 6.1 and 6.2 summarise the results obtained from the question:

In the last seven days how many times has your husband or partner:

made a meal for the family?
'cleared away' after a meal?
washed clothes for the family?
done general housework?
ironed clothes?
made beds?

This question appeared at the end of the questionnaire and was based on some of the interviews conducted. Rather than an impressionistic response to the idea of domestic labour being performed by men I wanted information on the actual domestic activities undertaken by them. Given the repetitive nature of much of this work asking how many times such tasks had been performed by husbands or partners in the previous seven days seemed the most appropriate way of obtaining this information. The tasks themselves deliberately range from the archetypal 'clearing away after a meal' through the repetitive 'unskilled' general housework to the semi-skilled work involved in ironing and washing, and the skilled 'making a meal'. Where prompts were necessary it was pointed out that 'making a meal' was understood to involve preparation and cooking, rather than the 'heating up' of previously prepared or tinned foods.

As Figure 6.1 illustrates, apart from 'clearing away' after a meal, perhaps the archetypal domestic labour activity engaged in by males (over 40 per cent had 'cleared away' four times or more), almost 60 per cent of husbands/partners had done no general housework and almost 70 per cent had not made a meal in the previous seven days. Figure 6.2 shows the percentage of husbands/partners who had ironed or washed clothes and made beds in the last seven days. The results provide a similar picture to that of Figure 6.1. Over 90 per cent had not made beds and 60 per cent and more had not been involved in either washing or ironing clothes. Such findings are broadly similar to those of Brannen and Moss:

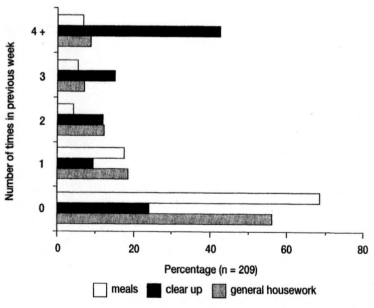

Figure 6.1 Male participation in domestic labour

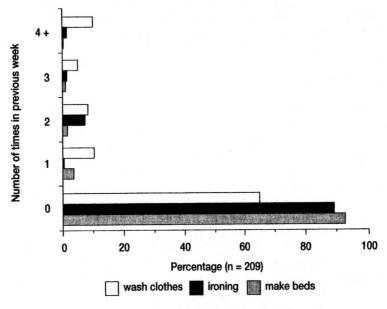

Figure 6.2 Male participation in domestic labour 2

Fathers were most likely to contribute to household shopping and clearing away after meals; 40–60 per cent did these tasks at least weekly (for shopping) or most days (for clearing away). Their contribution was lower on the other tasks, particularly preparing meals, ironing and washing clothes ... Non-employed mothers scored higher on the total domestic work score than mothers in dual earner households; this difference held when households with 'domestic help' were excluded ... Fathers in dual earner households were also reported to do all tasks more frequently than fathers with non-employed partners ... [Nevertheless] ... Although our data shows that men with employed partners did more 'family work' than those without, the most striking reality was that on every indicator studied, mothers with full-time jobs did the main part of this work.

(Brannen and Moss, 1991:175–177, 179)

These results will, of course, come as no surprise to those familiar with the work completed by researchers adopting a broadly feminist perspective. Many of the researchers mentioned above have provided ample evidence that points to the burden of domestic labour as one of the principle features maintaining the gender divisions in the experience of leisure. For example, Green *et al.* argue that

> Other studies have similarly found that married women's employment, whether part-time and temporary or professional and permanent, is not associated with any significant redistribution of housework tasks or domestic responsibilities from the traditional sexual division of labour (see for example Young and Wilmott, 1973; Edgell, 1980; Hunt, 1980; 1986a).

(Green et al., 1990:93)

To what extent, however, can variations be observed with regard to the backgrounds and educational levels of respondents similar to those that have already been discovered? Given our observations of the fragmentary nature of the new middle class, and the differences in experience between households associated with professional occupations and higher educational qualifications compared to those associated with managerial occupations and lower educational qualifications, might not differences in the gendering of domestic labour be observed here? Table 6.6 reproduces the responses to the question on p. 105, but in the context of the social background and educational level of males.

Table 6.6 The habitus and male participation in domestic labour (percentage) (n = 185)

Habitus	Wash 1+	Meal 3+	Meal None	Iron 1+	Clear 3+	Clear None	Beds 3+	Beds None
1 w/c low ed. (n = 49)	6	13	61	7	49	28	11	61
2 w/c high ed. (n = 32)	15	20	54	23	50	35	23	46
3 m/c low ed. (n = 54)	4	15	52	7	54	23	14	69
4 m/c high ed. (n = 50)	12	8	42	25	80	4	29	50

Notes: See Table 6.1

Although the figures indicate primarily that it is women who are mainly responsible for this domestic labour, they do support some of the distinctions associated with social origin and educational level that we have previously discovered. With only two minor exceptions associated with 'making a meal' and 'clearing away' for men in category 3, (m/c low ed.), it is invariably those with the highest education, categories 2 and 4, that are most likely to have participated in domestic labour. When one remembers the earlier relationships suggested by this type of analysis, particularly the relationship between this variable and the occupations of both males and females, clearly these results suggest that it is in the more highly educated, professional households where both partners are most likely to be working that domestic labour is shared more evenly. Even here, however, it is invariably women who take the responsibility for such labour. Again our findings coincide with the work by Brannen and Moss on dual-earner households.

The evidence does suggest that mothers in 'high status' occupations or with partners in such jobs did rather less domestic work and that fathers, by implication, took a rather greater share – at least in dual earner households.

(Brannen and Moss, 1991:183)

In their study of women who return to work after the birth of children, *Managing Mothers*, Brannen and Moss developed a 'domestic work score' from their data analysis (1991:175). The 'score' is associated with male performance of domestic tasks similar to those in this study: housework, preparing meals, washing clothes and ironing. Again women were asked to indicate how often their partners engaged in such tasks. From a maximum possible score of 28 the 'mothers' in Brannen and Moss's study scored on average 19.4. The figures for those families without 'domestic help', the vast majority, were higher (20) than those few with domestic help (14.9). In virtually all cases these working mothers engaged in significantly more domestic labour than their partners, although the working mothers did less than those who were not in full-time employment outside the home.

Similarly, in Chapter 10 of *Divisions of Labour* (1984), Pahl goes to considerable lengths in constructing his DOMDIV (division of domestic labour) classification. Based on extensive fieldwork, this classification is an attempt to measure the degree of participation in domestic labour by gender. It is particularly complex and overarching in that it attempts to measure the aggregate participation scores for the sample and then, through a series of controls, offers indications of domestic labour participation according to a series of variables such as position in the occupational structure for males and females, family life cycle and ages of children. As one would expect in a society in which membership of the paid labour force overwhelmingly discriminates against women, and one in which certain tasks, such as child-rearing, are still predominantly considered a female activity, the households that Pahl examined made use of a series of strategies which reflect and help reproduce this state of affairs. Not surprisingly Pahl discovered that the life cycle, particularly that part associated with child-rearing and non-paid employment amongst women, results in DOMDIV scores that show that females are engaged in considerably greater domestic labour activity than their male spouses or partners. Unfortunately, as Deem points out,

> Pahl's analysis of the Isle of Sheppey material, after all this, still allows him to say little more than that 'it is overwhelmingly obvious that women do most of the work in the household' [Pahl, 1985:270].

(Deem, 1986:76)

It is apparent, both from my own data and that of other research examined here, that domestic labour, in spite of participation in the paid labour force, is still predominantly understood as a gendered activity primarily undertaken by females. When one removes what might be described as 'singular productive activity in domestic provisioning' – the kind of activity that although regular is relatively infrequent in the domestic labour cycle, such as home decorating and structural maintenance, the kind of domestic labour activity more associated with males – the relationship between domestic labour and gender is even stronger. For the most part it is women rather than men who take responsibility for the day in, day out, domestic labour activities. And even when men regularly participate in such tasks, the managerial schedules are inevitably set by women.

The following material is taken from three interviews conducted with women. Together they illustrate a range of approaches and positions with regard to gender and domestic labour, but nevertheless show how the *responsibility* for housework resides with the woman in each case.

110

The first interviewee, Joan, left school at 16 with three O levels. She has had a variety of full- and part-time jobs and currently works part-time as a sales representative for a cosmetics company. She and her husband (an engineer for Shell Petrochemicals) have two teenage children.

Dave's good in the house – he'll do anything I ask and he always washes up. He'll do the shopping if I give him a list, and he always helped with the children when they were younger – putting them to bed, reading stories, bathtime and so on. Sometimes he'll wash clothes, like his sports kit, but not iron, he doesn't know how. As you know we're both very keen squash players and we help organise the teams – we're both out quite often, some weeks every night between us, what with playing and organising we sometimes see very little of each other. My work is really for the extras – I quite enjoy it part-time, Dave sometimes says I should give it up if I want to, but it helps with things like holidays or whatever.

The following interview material neatly illustrates a point made by Deem. In her study she found that women not in paid employment

were the most likely to have organised their housework into a routine, which both structured their day and possibly allowed them a small amount of space for themselves.

(Deem, 1986:90)

Pat does not work outside the home, and has not done so since her children were born. She left school at 15 with no formal qualifications. Prior to the birth of her children she worked as a secretary/clerical assistant for a food distribution company. Her husband Peter is a senior manager in a medium-sized engineering company.

I'm pretty organised as far as housework is concerned. Peter? – oh no, well I'm sure he would if I asked, if I needed him to, but he works hard and I see housework as my area, to keep the home. Of course there's a plan, different things get done on different days, a bit like the old saying 'Mondays is wash days . . . ' and so on. It's mainly all done in the mornings – with shopping in the afternoons.

There's no fixed routine as far as breakfast is concerned. Peter leaves at around 7.30 on most days and makes some tea for me before he leaves. I'll be up by eight and then do one of the main jobs – washes are at least three each week, then it all has to be pressed and ironed. Dusting, vacuum and general cleaning on two mornings. Then there are beds, windows and floors – it is a full-time job if it's done properly. I really don't see how some people can manage – those who are working.

We'll go to some of the social events but usually we go somewhere else at weekends, a country restaurant, or maybe into Chester or Manchester, it depends on who we are with.

Julie is a secondary schoolteacher of biology and is married to Tony, a civil engineer. Both have been educated beyond degree level. They have two children at the local junior school.

Housework? I do as little as possible, in some ways I suppose I'm not a wife at all in the traditional sense. Some days Tony will cook – it depends on who's home first – I'll pull something out of the freezer in the morning before I go to work and whoever gets back first starts it off. In the week we eat at around 6.30 – 7.30. Now the kids are a little older they look after themselves when they get home but of course they know that they can always go to Barbara or Helen [homes of close neighbours/ friends] with any problems. I'm usually back myself by 5.30, or Tony is so that's not really a problem. All the housework gets done on either Saturdays or Sundays. Apart from that in term time I'm just too busy – as you can see [looking around the room] it's not a priority [laughs].

We both play a lot of squash, and I play tennis so that's how we spend a lot of our leisure time, and of course all the socials and parties with the tennis. Tony is more likely to stay for a drink [at the clubhouse after squash] than I am, I sometimes stay but in the week I'm just too tired.

The corollary of the domestic labour arrangements illustrated above can be seen in Figure 6.3 which shows the responses to the question:

In the last seven days how many times has your husband/partner:

'gone out' in the evening for two hours or more?
played a sport or engaged in a leisure activity with someone other than yourself or your children?

Here it is worth noting that almost 40 per cent of the respondents' husbands/partners had 'gone out' in the evening at least once for two hours or more and 23 per cent had 'gone out' in the evening on more than one occasion. Similarly, almost 55 per cent had engaged in a sporting or leisure activity with someone other than their wife/partner and almost 30 per cent had done so on more than one occasion. For males, domestic labour is clearly a minority activity and leisure practices would appear to be under little constraint for the men in this sample. The extent to which this is indeed the case will, of course, be important in shaping and constructing the nature of the leisure practices available to both

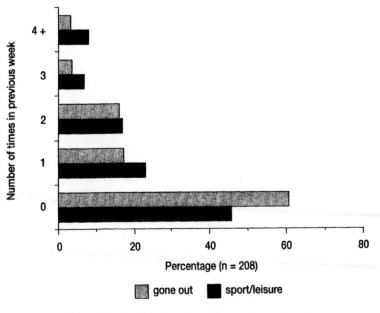

Figure 6.3 Husband/partner: leisure in past week

males and females on The Heath. In short, if leisure practices are dominated by men, then the shape and structure of those practices will, of course, reflect their own interests. As Green *et al.* point out in their review of previous research,

> A key point that emerges from feminist theories of social control and available empirical data, is the extent to which male social control of women is unexceptional; *it is a part of normal everyday life* ... This has clear implications for how, when and where women spend their leisure time and is a major factor in promoting and perpetuating gender inequalities in leisure.
>
> (Green *et al.*, 1990:101; my emphasis)

Dempsey's research into the social organisation of a sports club in a Sydney suburb illustrates this point. He shows that it is the men's agenda that dominates, leaving women to act in subservient roles as 'servicers' of the men – providing teas and lunches and cleaning and serving in the sports club bar (Dempsey, 1988). In our study women played an essentially similar role for the men's squash team. One requirement of entry into the league in which the squash teams played was the provision of a cooked meal after matches. It was invariably the wives of male players who provided these meals, whereas for the women's squash team such meals were always provided by the players themselves – to the extent that certain matches were rearranged in order to ensure that a meal could be provided. Green *et al.* make the same point:

> Women's housework and childcare responsibilities do not fit neatly into a conventional working day, and many women are almost constantly 'on call', which makes it difficult to plan leisure in advance with any degree of certainty.
>
> (Green *et al.*, 1990:25)

Further support for this theory can be found in the very way in which access to certain facilities is made available. For example, in the use of the squash courts at The Heath's clubhouse a fortnightly timetable, with one week changed on a weekly basis, is used for residents to book squash courts in advance. A complicated system of rules applies to ensure that individuals do not abuse the system by 'overbooking' courts for themselves. These restrictions include a mixture of 'prime time' limitations on the booking of courts and a maximum number of courts that are 'bookable' by individuals in the first few days of a 'new' week. In attempting to produce a 'fair' system for all this system mitigates against female use because women find it more difficult to plan their own leisure because of the nature and demands of domestic labour. Interviews with women about their use of the squash facility invariably produced comments such as,

> 'It's so difficult to book a court.'
> 'Whenever we look to get a court the times that we can make always seem to be booked.'
> 'It's impossible! The men get over there as soon as the booking sheets go up – leave it for a couple of days and you'll find that playing before 10 pm is impossible.'

Such remarks are reproduced in the statistics on women's use of the clubhouse squash facilities in Table 6.7 below. By contrast the numbers of women who use the swimming pool are considerably higher and show little difference with that of men's usage. Similar findings were made by Green et al. (1987). On this point, however, Green et al. (1990), in offering an explanation as to why mothers appear to have more opportunities for sport than childless wives, suggest,

> it may be that much of a mother's physical recreation is not so much independent leisure as family leisure. Given the popularity of swimming, for example, it could be that what we are counting as instances of women's participation in sport may in practice be mothers' opportunities to spend an hour bent double in lukewarm water helping their children to swim!
>
> (Green et al., 1990:68)

The use of The Heath's swimming pool for three hours on Sunday mornings for children's 'learn to swim classes' may reflect this state of affairs.

The recreational facilities of The Heat may be used in such a way that in part, at least, the rules and 'practices of use' (de Certeau, 1984) associated with them come to reflect a gendered definition of appropriate use. Having established such definitional practices the use of these facilities will then come to reflect these definitions (see Chapter 7).

As we discovered in the previous chapter when we examined leisure and sporting practices and the use of The Heath's clubhouse facilities there are significant differences between respondents. In summarising our discussion of these data (Tables 5.2 and 5.3), we concluded that The Heath's clubhouse facilities were an important defining characteristic and helped form and maintain lifestyle distinctions between residents according to their social origins, educational level and occupation. By paying closer attention to female participation we can examine both the differences in men's and women's participation patterns and, indeed, some of the variation within women's participation itself. Table 6.7 below brings together some of the data examined previously but specifically presented to show these differences.

The table shows that the greatest variations between males and females appear to occur in attending the clubhouse for a drink, and in playing squash. The use of the swimming pool and tennis courts do not appear to be differentiated by gender, although a slightly greater percentage of women respondents appear to play tennis. It should be remembered that these figures refer to the most frequent users of these facilities, defined in terms of their use/attendance on at least three occasions each month.

As in our previous analyses it is perhaps more interesting to consider the differences between women according to their social origins and educational levels. When differences in use and participation with regard to these elements of the habitus are examined, further support for the thesis of fragmentation is discovered. With regard to the squash and tennis facilities it is the women of working-class origin and the highest educational levels who are most likely to use these facilities, whereas it is the women with the lowest educational levels, irrespective of social origin, who are least likely to play tennis or squash and most likely to attend social activities and to drink regularly at the clubhouse. When we remember that the structure of the households on The Heath shows considerable homogeneity with regard to the educational levels and social origins of partners (Table 6.1), the above data further supports the fragmentary thesis, suggesting that these divisions also cut across the gendered use of the clubhouse and its recreational facilities.

Table 6.7 The habitus and aspects of women's leisure (n = 179)

Social origin and education capital		Attending social activity at clubhouse		Social event elsewhere with partner	Drink at clubhouse		Swim at clubhouse		Squash at clubhouse		Tennis at clubhouse	
		female	male		female	male	female	male	female	male	female	male
All	often	22	21	25	14	22	33	34	17	30	29	25
w/c high ed. (n = 28)	often	21	22	17	17	22	35	40	26	40	40	39
m/c high ed. (n = 28)	often	13	11	26	8	20	27	35	12	36	23	27
w/c low ed. (n = 49)	often	34	38	13	42	33	40	30	9	20	23	15
w/c high ed. (n = 28)	often	32	30	43	33	25	27	32	9	25	24	19

Notes: See Table 6.1

CONCLUSION: THE SOCIAL SPACE OF GENDER AND THE HOUSEHOLD

Figure 6.4, like Figures 4.1 and 5.9 provides a representation of the social space of the new middle class with regard to gender and the household. As with our previous analyses the suggestion is one of a developing fragmentation within this new middle class rather than homogeneity and when examined alongside the previous diagrams it suggests a set of homologies which incorporate gendered differences within this fragmentation.

In many ways our analysis of the domestic household on The Heath has revealed little that was not already known from previous research. Broadly the findings with regard to domestic

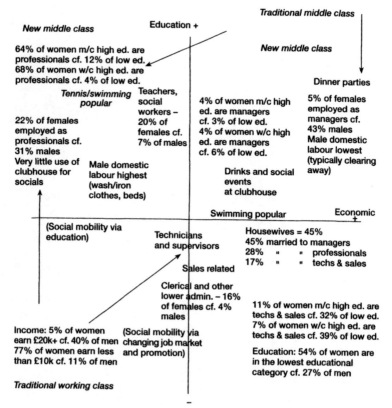

Figure 6.4 The social space of gender

provisioning, gender and domestic labour, and gender and leisure are similar to previous investigations. Like these earlier investigations both our quantitative and qualitative data reveal that it is primarily women rather than their male partners who plan and manage the day-to-day work activities in the household and it is primarily women who accomplish these tasks.

Unlike some of the previous research, differences have been observed with regard to the divisions previously established within our sample, namely social origin and educational level, and the associated occupations of both males and females. As far as domestic labour is concerned it is men and women in those households with members educated to degree level, irrespective of social origin, who are most likely to share domestic tasks. When we recall the relationship between education and occupation it further suggests that it is primarily amongst professionals that domestic labour is most likely to be shared. Previous research that has examined dual income families, such as the work of Brannen and Moss, is further supported by our findings which suggest that it is women who work outside the home who are most likely to share domestic tasks with partners.

Leisure spaces also indicate strong gender differentiation associated with their construction. Features of social life associated with the use of the recreational facilities indicate that The Heath and the new middle classes living there construct social lives in which gender provides an important differentiating characteristic. However, in looking at the use of The Heath's clubhouse and sports facilities, our data suggest that the gendered differentials observed are modified with regard to the social origin, educational level and occupation of both the respondent and the household in which the respondent is located. Clearly, while much of the use of the clubhouse and sports facilities is associated more with males than females, the relationships discovered earlier are maintained, though to a lesser degree amongst females. In short, although the differences between females are less apparent, they do nevertheless exist. When one remembers the importance of work outside the home in giving women 'the right' to leisure (Deem, 1986), then it is perhaps the status of housewife that accounts for some of the differences observed. Here, however, it should be noted that such a status is itself a part of the wider fragmentation of the new middle class and can be mapped onto those divisions (Figure 6.4).

In conclusion, then, while we have been able to document significant differences in the leisure lifestyles of men and women it must be remembered that such differences impinge upon women quite differently according to, in our analysis, their social origins, educational qualifications and occupations. Such an analysis questions those who would argue a position based on the 'essentiality' of a 'common world of women' associated with some of the feminist researches examined above. As Rojek has recently argued,

> there are dangers in accepting the 'common world' view at face value. Much research shows that differences in status, class and type of household affect women's subjective experience of leisure (Glyptis *et al.* 1987; Bolla *et al.* 1991).
>
> (Rojek, 1995:32)

Similarly, while the majority of women in our study of the new middle class(es) can be seen to operate under similar constraints with regard to domestic labour, and while differences in constraints and opportunities can also be related to occupation, child care and the life cycle, nevertheless important differences *between* women can be observed. Further, such differences can be seen to relate to the principal concerns of our argument, namely the cultural fragmentation and heterogeneity of the new middle class(es).

7

THE CLUBHOUSE

The clubhouse and other facilities that exist for the exclusive use of residents of The Heath provide one of the most salient characteristics for understanding the social lives of residents. It is the practices of use and non-use of these facilities that distinguish them from each other and which serve the residents themselves with the material with which to identify each other.

The property development company responsible for The Heath felt that in order to ensure a market for its development facilities in addition to the houses themselves would be needed. While the ease of motorway and rail connections were selling points the surrounding villages offered little other than solitude and country walks. Local library facilities were poor, schools relatively small and post offices and local shops were virtually non-existent. Sports facilities, apart from one small tennis club, a golf course and village playing fields, were also lacking. For the most part, the indigenous local community is best characterised as rural, with a work force closely associated with arable and dairy farming and sand quarrying. Having said this, a dormitory estate had been developed in one of the two closest villages, some 2 miles away, and a small country town was able to cater for most of the needs of the surrounding population. Significant centres of population exist to both the east and north west, less than an hour's drive away, and many of The Heath's residents are employed or have businesses in these locations. However, as far as daily life is concerned there is little outside of The Heath itself to which residents would be attracted. As such, the development of inclusive leisure facilities became a major marketing tool of the property development company. In addition, due to the pressure on amenities and resources provided by the local council, the developer's idea to provide such self-contained leisure facilities helped ensure the necessary planning permission for the estate. Interviews with the company chairman and senior employees of the property company also revealed an interest in producing a residential facility similar to those found in parts of North America. The company chairman, an archetypal self-made man, revealed a concern to provide something different from competitors, together with a desire to 'make a statement' for his company. Background research at the initial stages of the investigation revealed the existence of few other developments of this type. What did exist was either much smaller or approached the far larger developments associated with the 'new town' movement of the London satellites and Milton Keynes. No single private developer had yet attempted to produce a development similar to The Heath, although subsequently several have been developed. Although the marketing materials suggested the creation of a 'traditional village community', initial house purchase prices and the continued maintenance of their commercial values has ensured that The Heath is available to only the most affluent of first-time buyers.

On purchasing a house on The Heath one also contracts shared ownership of the communal facilities and a contractual obligation for their upkeep. Payments for this are made on an annual basis either through a single payment or monthly order.

LEISURE PRACTICES AND SOCIAL IDENTITY

Leisure practices are the principal ways in which residents of The Heath mark themselves from one another. They are the primary practices in which the work of 'distinction' is accomplished between different social groups, and the practices by which individuals come to identify with others. Lest this description suggests a positive flurry of activity by all and sundry, it should be noted that non-engagement, as much as engagement, can be seen as a social practice important to 'distinction'. In addition, the 'style' of non-engagement is also important in processes of distinction in the sense that a *disinterested* mode carries a differentiated meaning to a non-engagement based upon a challenged rejection of certain practices. Here we can note an important distinction between the positive boycotting of an event because it does not conform to one's wishes and a non-engagement based upon *disinterestedness*. Such differences are immediately apparent in the interview material reproduced below which records responses made to questions about the use of the clubhouse facilities.

> I don't believe these facilities should be used by people who are not residents of The Heath – apart from the occasional guest. Yet the very existence of the teams requires this. It's just not right, and certainly not in keeping with idea of exclusive facilities for residents. And of course it means that with these teams it becomes impossible to get a court for the occasional game. There are plenty of tennis clubs in this area for people . . . just a lack of consideration for other residents.

> We have very little to do with the club. We certainly don't play any sports and hardly ever use the bar there. I spend a lot of time travelling, and I'm sure Elizabeth has no need of any of these facilities. We like the countryside and the quiet but the facilities are irrelevant to us. Most of our friends live elsewhere and when we do get together with friends for dinner or the theatre or whatever . . . [it's] usually far away from here.

The clubhouse recreational facility available to all residents and charged to each household on an annual basis is the principle site around which distinctions have emerged on The Heath. Originally managed by the property developers, this facility was 'handed' to an elected residents committee approximately three years after the development had begun, at which time some 250 properties were occupied. Prior to this an elected residents committee had acted as 'advisors' to the development company on matters regarding the development and maintenance of the clubhouse and sports facilities. One of these representatives explained his role to me thus:

> The trustees ensure that the facilities are maintained adequately, that the landscaped areas are kept up and that the place is generally treated with the respect it deserves – and most people are perfectly accepting of that. We have very few problems with non-payers, it's not that kind of place, is it, after all given the house prices, and the cost of golf club fees now-

adays, the fees here are pretty minimal – and remember it includes the whole family. There was one occasion when a group of people attempted to introduce fee paying for using the facilities – their argument was that maintenance would obviously increase the more the facilities were used and therefore the users should pay. Happily their efforts were defeated, although we have introduced fees for use of the lights for tennis and squash.

 As others have noted elsewhere (Bracey, 1964; Bell, 1968), the voluntary association has become one of the hallmark characteristics of the middle class, ranging from village clubs and societies to international aid and care organisations: on The Heath it is voluntary associations that have emerged to take control of the management of the facilities. These associations have developed as a way of managing the physical spaces and recreational opportunities provided by the clubhouse. At the same time other associations, primarily concerned with child care, hobbies and pastimes, have been formed by residents. To date there are at least six voluntary associations which serve to manage and co-ordinate The Heath's facilities. These include user groups and associations for the following activities: social events committee, squash, tennis, youth club, mother and toddler group and aerobics.

While participation in these associations is potentially available to all, it is clear in the development of these groupings that they exhibit considerable powers in defining the social practices that construct the particular activities that they are associated with. Furthermore, such practices serve to identify how certain activities should be undertaken, how the physical and social spaces of the facilities are interrelated and how inclusion and exclusion of residents in particular groupings is accomplished. As such the incorporation of residents into the various associations and, therefore, their participation in the sports and leisure facilities available, produces a complex web of relationships through which residents identify themselves to others. Further, it is through the development of these associations, known as 'user groups' that 'legitimate' participation is developed. The interview material below relates to the development of the tennis and squash 'user groups' and indicates how the 'legitimating practices' of such groups have initiated certain conflicts amongst residents, hinted at in the trustee's reference to the introduction of fees for tennis and squash lighting.

When we first moved here very few people played, in fact no one really played tennis, apart from a few people with their children – but it wasn't really playing tennis. Then Helen and I were playing one day and a couple came onto the other court and began to knock up. It was obvious, I'm sure he won't mind me saying this, obvious that he had not really been coached, whereas Jane [his wife] obviously had. It's very easy to tell with tennis whether someone's been coached – you can even tell when they were coached to the nearest five years or so . . . all to do with changes in the game, more top spin and wrist today, less slice. Anyway Jim played a lot of squash and was very fit so his enthusiasm and eye for a ball meant that he could give his wife a reasonable game. We met afterwards in the bar and began talking about how no one used the courts and arranged to play with them. Within a few months Jim's game had improved tremendously and more and more people began to use the courts. By this time three or four others were obviously reasonable players and we began a men's four – every Sunday morning rain or shine and carried it on into the winter. By that time there were two men's fours going and Jim had made some inquiries about a winter league which we joined. After that it just took off and now we have two men's and two women's fours in the leagues, winter and summer. In the beginning you just turned up and played, but now we have a booking system for the courts – copied from the squash really. In fact I think there are as many if not more people playing tennis than there are squash.

The teams have become a bit of an issue over the years because of the lights and the time that they take. Some people argue that the facilities should be available to residents only, but of course when we play league matches the opposition is obviously from elsewhere. The thing is the majority of people here don't play anyway and I don't see why we should have to give up the teams just on the off chance that others might want to use the courts. Before we started no one played at all – it was the same with squash.

The only way this place makes money is through what passes over there [the bar]. Without us everyone would be paying more fees, so I don't see why those who play tennis and squash shouldn't pay some extra. Swimming is different, that's for the kids, you know learning to swim and so on. Other things, well you can't charge for everything can you?

The previous chapters have identified different leisure experiences associated with a heterogeneity in the sample discovered in our analysis of social origin, educational background and occupation in Chapter 4. In Figure 4.1, 'The social space of mobility' it was shown that the occupational structure within the new middle class could be differentiated according to social origin and educational capital. Different 'mobility paths' were identified for both the traditional working and middle classes which indicated that divisions between managerial and professional workers, technicians and the self-employed were apparent. Our developing model also indicated that gender differences and income levels were also associated with these divisions. In Chapter 5 the model was further developed to show some of the recreational and non-work differences between these social groupings (Figure 5.9). Of particular interest for this study were the observed differences in the use of the clubhouse facilities – the use of the clubhouse bar (drinkers) and participation in social events, and the use of the sports facilities (sporters). For the most part the former could be identified as being primarily associated with those of working-class origins and the least amounts of educational capital, and the latter with those of working-class origin and the highest amounts of educational capital. However, at the end of Chapter 5 we argued that in addition to the statistical representation an analysis of the 'practices of use' associated with these facilities was required. The statistical observations that have identified the homologies between social origin, educational capital, occupational position, leisure and recreational practices need to be located in the social construction of the everyday lives of our sample if we are to show how these divisions are both structured by and structuring of social position. How is the clubhouse bar and how are the sports facilities used by our identified social groupings in order that these facilities, and their use, become a 'part' of that which allows for (and produces) both the identification of them by others and their own identification practices? In short, how does the legitimate and legitimating use of these facilities become a part of the habitus of these groupings. In the description and analysis which follows, the case study material looks at some of the more general features associated with the leisure lifestyles of these groupings and examines their use of the recreational facilities on The Heath.

Observational notes and case study material on the leisure lifestyles of the grouping 'drinkers' indicates a series of preferences that Bourdieu finds amongst the French *petite bourgeoisie*. This group exhibits a preference for the hotel-based family holiday in the Mediterranean or North America at the height of summer; weekends away at country hotels; horse-racing; football matches and a minority interest in golf, although this is played on occasional visits to a variety of clubs, rather than as a member of a specific club. Eating out is a favoured weekend activity, although choice of restaurant is primarily the steak house.

In the home emphasis is placed on comfort and tidiness rather than design and homes are furnished with the 'solid' furniture of the established company – heavily upholstered and cushioned, fitted carpeting and 'heavy' curtains. Visits to the theatre or cinema are rare, the video is more popular, but when taken such visits are usually to see the spectacular film or star vehicle, and theatre visits are to see shows and musicals at venues such as the Palace in Manchester, a favourite venue for promoters of West End productions. With respect to such visits, it is not uncommon for members of this group to organise a 'coach party' to attend the latest musical revival or other 'off The Heath' entertainment. One example was an outing to a Liverpool brewery, arranged by someone who worked for a company that had supplied the brewery with electrical fittings. What was initially understood to be a tour of the company and the production process became an evening of entertainment: free drinks, food and live music in one of the brewery company's executive suites.

In comparison with some of the leisure activities engaged in by other residents, in this group membership of voluntary associations is small and no one who was spoken to had ever been invited or expressed a desire to join any of the groups created by other residents, such as the gardening club or those associated with the sports facilities. In spite of the fact that their children make up many of the members of the young residents club, only two adults were members of the 'help rota' created for the club's supervision.

By contrast, the second grouping, 'sporters', exhibits what Featherstone has termed 'a learning mode to life . . . consciously educating [themselves] in the field of taste, style, [and] lifestyle' (Featherstone, 1987:65). Their homes are more likely to exhibit style than comfort: the leather chesterfield or sofa grouping, rather than the three-piece suite; the feature coffee table and magazine rack, even the magazines themselves; parquet or tiled flooring, rather than the fitted carpet; component hi-fi rather than the 'one piece enclosed system' and associated record collections of a particular style of music rather than compilations of popular music or established classics. Holiday taste is à la carte, a *gîte* or campsite in France rather than the a travel company package.

Instead of the 'star vehicle' or musical, 'sporters' are more likely to attend the established or avant-garde theatre, associated in Manchester with the Royal Exchange or Cornerhouse. The adoption of a learning mode to their leisure activities can be seen in their attendance at evening classes to take courses in foreign languages, musical or artistic appreciation and games such as bridge. Other indicators relate to their membership of the voluntary associations that they have been primarily responsible for creating, such as the clubs associated with the sports facilities, the care of children, and the swimming and aerobics clubs.

A NIGHT AT THE CLUB: 'DRINKERS'

In the clubhouse bar at 6.15 pm one evening six or seven people can be seen either standing or seated at the bar, the early evening drinkers stopping off 'for a quick one' on their way home from work. Significantly all are male and include some well-known regulars – Kevin, Jonesy, Alec, Neil and Phil.

Phil is an airline steward and was not working today – he had been playing squash with Helen, a regular partner who had left for home after a 'quick drink'. It emerged later that her husband Daniel was playing 'first team squash' away from home and she felt that she ought to be at home before he left to play. Tonight

Neil, a businessman from southern England in his late thirties, managing director of a plastics moulding company, was bemoaning the difficulties of raising venture capital in the UK compared with the rest of Europe. Neil can be found in the bar on most weekday evenings between 6 and 7 pm, sometimes staying until closing time, in which case his wife usually joins him at around 9.30 pm, or he will leave and return with his wife later. Neil's primary use of the facilities on The Heath is his regular drinking in the bar, as it is with the other men mentioned above. Although he plays the occasional game of squash such games are relatively infrequent compared to those played by members of the 'sporting clique'. Indeed this is not our categorisation but rather one that is offered by the 'drinkers' in their own conversations when categorising other residents of The Heath.

The conversation moved from one topic to another with apparent ease and Phil, taking his cue from the mention of other European countries, began describing the problems associated with airline discounting methods, how cheap seats are obtained, which destinations and flight times are most likely to be available and how they may be taken advantage of. He works for a major airline and regularly flies to all parts of the world spending a considerable amount of time away from home. These trips always seem to produce incidents which he gregariously relates to his drinking friends on his return. He is happy to be defined by them as an 'all-action male' engaged in a series of escapades associated with his work – expenses paid hotels, duty-free goods and 'fake' Rolex watches which are made available to his friends in this clique – and when 'home' he can be found in the bar on most evenings. Phil has lived on The Heath for over ten years and is recognised as one of the stalwarts of the drinking clique. Like other 'scousers' living on The Heath Phil has been instrumental in maintaining certain traditions associated with being a member of the drinking clique, such as the male dominated rituals of pool competitions, Saturday lunchtime drinking and the provision of TV in the bar for major sporting events. Whenever a pool competition is taking place or a 'book' is run on events such as the Grand National, Phil, more often than not, will have some involvement with it.

Alec too is strongly identified with this clique, although in a different way. For the clique Alec performs a role as something of a mascot. He is guaranteed regularly to have drunk more than he should, to stay in the bar, when, by his own admission he ought to be at home, to be impervious to suggestions that he should be any different than he is and identified as someone always willing to talk or rather to listen painlessly to what anyone else might wish to say. Although Alec does not enjoy either the occupational status or income of some of the drinking clique, these potential difficulties are overcome by the fact that he is somewhat older than most of the others, enjoys a stable family life and is able to regale the rest with stories of his matriarchal household, run, as he sees it, by his wife and two teenage daughters. He keeps his position in the clique by his longevity, his willingness to defer in argument to others, his legendary drinking activity and the occasional story of 'hound dog' shopping trips with his family. Nothing is discussed intently and virtually everyone has something to say about any topic that another mentions.

It is noticeable that every time the club door opened heads were turned to discover who might be arriving. Suitable candidates were invited to join the group with appropriate signals, a raised hand or eye contact in recognition and welcome, an exclamation of someone's arrival with comments such as 'Here he comes' or 'What's kept you?' or an immediate offer with 'What are you having?' On some occasions not even such greetings are necessary as it will be obvious to the group of 'drinkers' that this new arrival will join them and his 'drink' will be provided without anyone asking what he would like. In some cases the bar steward's knowledge of the group allows him to participate by simply serving the drink at the bar and waiting for one of the group to produce the money for payment. From knowledge of the group it is estimated that such status is conferred on around thirty males.

Anyone entering the bar at this time, known by the group as 'early doors', that the group does not consider appropriate company is ignored – the door opens, the group looks and then averts its gaze. During one typical observation period twelve arrivals were dealt with in this way within an hour.

One way in which the group solidifies relationships is in the collective finishing of drinks and 'the round'. Participants are encouraged to finish their drinks together so that 'the round' is not lost – should one or two be not quite ready then a sign of their collective belonging is to leave the drink 'in the pump' – a drink that has been paid for but not served. Standing one's round or being 'in a round' is a feature that allows for and produces collectivity and at the same time indicates to others not 'in the round' who is and is not excluded. As already stated, this form of entry to the group is not necessary as 'members' will be immediately included in a 'round' as soon as they enter the bar; for others, who exist on the periphery of a group, temporary or potential membership can be obtained by appropriate timing in the 'buying of a round'. Indeed potential 'members' are sometimes 'vetted' in this way. On some occasions a recognised drinker may bring a new neighbour or acquaintance to the bar and through the buying of drinks both he and members of the group have the opportunity to 'vet' each other.

Early evening drinking, 'early doors', and Saturday lunchtime drinking, as far as this group is concerned, is predominantly a male activity and only on very few occasions can women be observed. When this does happen, it only happens through the presence of a female partner (invariably a spouse) and the couple either drink together, somewhat apart from the group, or the group itself moves to the 'pool room'.

Later in the evenings, after around 9 pm, female partners (again invariably spouses) and other less frequent 'drinkers', together with other residents, can be found in the bar. Female partners of the most frequent male 'drinkers', can be found sitting at a table together, with the men stood at the bar. Such women rarely buy their own drinks, rather the round, held by the men, simply accommodates the women's drinks also. The women themselves only partially relate to the men and appear to have their own conversations without any obvious reference to that of their partners (husbands). From those conversations that have been overheard or reported to me, fashion, sex, holidays and eating out appear to be the main topics discussed, together with 'bitching' (their word not mine). In separate conversations with these women they said that 'bitching' or gossip about topics related to their husbands, neighbours and friends is not seen as a vindictive activity but rather as a series of petty moans which women share. Indeed concern is only expressed when another woman does not share the same 'petty moans'. This kind of social talk (conversation) rather than being understood as the expression of serious dissatisfaction appears to be a form of talk that is produced by, and is productive of, the establishment of common identities.

During one observational period in the bar during the middle

131

of the evening, four couples and two 'wives' joined an established 'drinking' group at around 9.30 pm and stayed until the bar closed. By 10 pm this group numbered approximately ten males and six females – all known to each other. Such a number, situated at the edge of the left corner of the bar, were unable to share a single conversation and split into one main group of males and females and two single sex groups. For most of the rest of the evening these interconnected groups were joined and left by their members. As this was a Monday evening, conversation included the weekend's activity – who had been out with whom, where to, and how much had been drunk. Two couples had been to a restaurant together and they told the others how they had danced with each other during the evening. Another couple had spent a 'quiet Saturday in' but stressed that this was unusual and that they had found themselves visited by another couple with whom they had 'finished Saturday evening/Sunday morning drinking Hine brandy' – stressing the name of the drink to let everyone know that they knew and could afford the best.

In examining the use of the lounge bar in the recreational complex, observation work clearly indicates that it is these 'drinkers' who are predominant in the production of this social space. The group is comprised of both sexes but is primarily constructed by the practice of 'male only drinking' on returning 'home' from work. As we have seen, this session develops shortly after opening at 5.30 pm on weekday evenings when a small but regular number of males enter the lounge bar. Their drinking is done at the bar itself, rather than at one of the tables, a practice that allows for the development of sociability amongst those who drink at this time. Joining a group standing at the bar is more easily accomplished than taking one's drink over to a table. When any of the tables are in fact occupied this is usually taken as a sign that those at such tables are engaged in conversational projects unsuited to the development of casual group drinking. The tables then, for those involved in these drinking practices, confer the status of privacy for those using them.

Conversation at the bar for 'the drinkers' might relate to the nature of the work day experienced, a review or preview of a national sporting event or conversation around an aspect of recent news. Such conversations tend not to be discursive, in the sense that varying points of view are expressed. Rather, such conversational work encourages the expression of commonly held beliefs with respect to either working practices, opinions on items of news or more general confirmatory talk regarding current concerns. This group tends to develop in size until about 7 pm after which the men tend to leave for dinner, returning later in the evening with their spouses and partners. By 10 pm many have returned and can be seen occupying similar positions at the bar to those they had vacated some two or three hours earlier. Sitting at tables close by are their spouses and partners. This gender segregation appears related to beliefs pertaining to what are deemed proper conversation and proper drinking practices for the sexes. Drinks are bought for all in turn but it is invariably the males who are responsible for purchasing these. Implicit in such practices are a set of normative expectations regarding gender roles (see Chapter 6).

For the most part members of this group do not avail themselves of the other recreational facilities of the complex. Most have not played a sport since leaving school and do not make regular use of the sports facilities available, apart from games of pool in a small room annexed from the bar. Indeed this room is almost the sole preserve of males belonging to this group.

It is suggested that members of this group are a *petite bourgeoisie* created from the ranks of the traditional working class whose advancement has occurred without the development of what Bourdieu terms cultural capital. Their position has developed primarily from the economic field and their leisure practices can be understood as an amplified version of those traditionally associated with the urban working class. Attendance at football matches is still important for some males, although they are more likely to be sitting in season-ticket stands or the executive boxes owned by companies, than the terraces they stood on as children. Other sporting events likely to be attended include golf matches, horse-racing, snooker and motor sports events but such visits are likely to be made via company 'complimentary tickets' rather than as enthusiasts for the particular sport. With respect to such visits, being at a sporting occasion is perhaps more important for the status it confers than for any intrinsic enjoyment of the sport itself.

The guarded animosity that exists between 'drinkers' and 'sporters' is illustrated in the conduct of the annual raffle for Wimbledon tickets run by the 'tennis section'. Affiliation to the Lawn Tennis Association provides the 'tennis section' with a number of tickets for the Wimbledon Championships and one way of raising funds to pay for 'match balls' and league affiliation fees is to hold a raffle for these tickets. However, in order to raise as large a sum as possible the purchase of such tickets is open to any member of the community. On two of the annual occasions when the 'draw' for these tickets has taken place both resulted in scenes of dismay and disgust amongst 'sporters' when the 'finals day' tickets were won by 'drinkers'. Muffled comments such as 'God, would you believe it!' and 'They don't deserve them' were drowned by shouts of glee as members of the 'drinking' group realised that the 'sporters' had failed to obtain one of the major rewards for their organisational efforts.

The leisure practice of this group that is most visible to other residents is its drinking, which is described by others as turning the bar into a 'working men's club'. Their preference for standing at the bar, ordering large rounds of drinks at 'last orders' and the sexual segregation practices associated with their drinking are evidenced by others as indicative of their social origins and the kind of people they are seen to be. Such drinking practices ensure a high visibility for this group of regular drinkers. They represent for less frequent and non-users 'what the bar is like', in that their domination of both the physical and social space of the lounge bar helps determine how the rest of the population use this facility. Some of the less frequent users have commented that the atmosphere in the bar reminds them of 'a posh working men's club'. Others have said that obtaining a drink at the bar is difficult because its whole length is always full with the same people – 'Why can't they sit at one of the tables and make it easier for everyone?'

Sitting at one of the tables, however, would present the 'drinkers' with a number of problems. As we have seen, this group develops during the course of the evening, beginning when the bar opens at 5.30 pm with male-only drinking. At this time men will mainly enter the bar alone, awaiting the arrival of other male drinking partners. Standing at the bar not only facilitates the serving of drinks by the steward but also allows for the development of the group via a series of 'recognition practices'. Later in the evening when mixed-sex company is the norm, males and females may be separated by the practice of the latter sitting at the nearest table to the bar. It is their utilisation of the bar frontage in this way that allows for, and is part of, their drinking practices.

In response to the views held of them, members of this group claim an authenticity for their actions which they deny to others. Those who don't engage in regular drinking are defined variously as being 'under the thumb', understood as wanting to but not being allowed to by family commitments, 'living in hock' – a reference usually to the size of a mortgage, financial commitments not allowing some to 'enjoy themselves', or 'miseries' – those who don't use the facilities yet complain about the behaviour of those who do. Such complaints are usually concerned with late drinking but also with the style of drinking referred to above. The 'drinkers' do not understand why anyone would buy a house on this estate and not avail themselves of this facility. Those who use the sports facilities but not the bar are seen as being unable to afford the drink that 'everyone needs after playing tennis or squash'! The 'drinkers' evaluate most 'sporters' as poseurs, recognising a similarity in their working-class origins and a realisation of the 'learning mode' in which 'sporters' are engaged, as expressed in such comments as 'They're just trying to be something they're not.'

For this group then social position is understood primarily in economic terms. It is constructed through an indulgence in activities associated with having more of the same rather than a reconstruction of lifestyle. The 'signs of arrival' associated with this group are the ability to pay cash rather than live on credit, to 'stand a round' without concerning oneself with the cost, to holiday abroad in a hotel rather than a tent, even if it is pitched for you, and generally to not have to worry about financial matters.

Such expressions are perhaps more embedded in certain aspects of respectable working-class, rather than middle-class culture. Their achievement has been a respectability by the standards of a working class that is fragmenting rather than a move into what one might term the new middle class. They look back with satisfaction to their social origins and regularly bring parents to the bar so that they too can be shown the successes of their children. A belief in hard work, and being in the right place at the right time, serves for them as an explanation of their material success.

SPORTING PRACTICES: 'SPORTERS'

By contrast, the most frequent users of the sports facilities could, in Bourdieu's terms, be said to relate more to the 'new

135

bourgeoisie'. The 'signs of arrival' associated with this group are related to how and what one plays and it is in this sense that we would argue that leisure is becoming increasingly important in the construction of their social position. The high visibility produced by the practices of the regular drinkers is replicated in the practices of the most frequent tennis and squash players. To understand the importance of these sporting practices it is necessary to examine their associated meanings, which as Bourdieu points out requires an examination of a variety of variables such as

How long ago, and how, the sport was learnt, how often it is played, the socially qualified conditions (place, time, facilities, equipment) and how it is played (position in a team, style etc.).

(Bourdieu, 1984:211)

Three areas of investigation help provide an understanding of the sporting practices associated with the playing of tennis and squash: team selection, clothing and equipment, and court management.

The Heath has four tennis teams which play in local tennis leagues. Three of these compete in the summer, two for men and one for women, and there is a winter team primarily composed of men, but which co-opts women on the relatively few occasions when not enough men are available to play. There are three squash teams, two for men and one for women. Although these numerical differences are understood by residents to reflect the demands they themselves make for competitive play, it is interesting to note that while quantitative data might support this belief with respect to squash, it does not do so for tennis, where in fact slightly more women than men play on a regular basis.

An indication of the importance of team selection and its role in sociability can be gained from the following conversation that took place in the lounge bar of the recreational facility. Three squash players were standing at the side of the bar opposite to that usually occupied by the 'regular drinkers'. Jon, Ray and Martin were talking about a forthcoming squash match in which Martin was unable to play. When asked why, he replied, 'I've got to be in a dinner jacket by eight-thirty.' This turned out to be a reference to a business evening in Liverpool which he needed to attend on the same night as the squash match. Ray and Jon then developed the conversation in terms of business meals they had eaten in various restaurants in the North West, each seemingly vying with the other to recount a story of more exclusivity and greater cost. The conversation then returned to the forthcoming squash match and in what follows we can gain some insight as to the importance attached to social position and sports ability. Jon, the team captain, informed Ray that he was considering playing him at number three rather than two, his usual position. In effect this was demotion for Ray who appeared 'put out' by this possibility. Jon informed him that Harry was currently playing well enough to beat him at the moment. Shortly after this Harry and his opponent came into the bar, and the following conversation ensued:

> JON: We'll see how Harry got on against Alan.
> RAY: If he beat him 3–0 then I'll worry.
> JON (to both players): What was the score?
> ALAN (Harry's opponent): We're not talking about the score.
> [This was correctly taken to be an indication that he had lost the match.]
> RAY: Three–love?
> (*Harry nodded his head in confirmation.*)
> RAY: Hmmmm.
> JON (*looking at Ray*): I told you.

Although moving down in the squash team ranking would not pose an immediate threat to Ray's membership of the team and the social scene afforded by such membership, should he find himself left out of matches for a period of time it would undoubtedly affect the quality of his wider social life with respect to the opponents he would then be playing against, and therefore the social group he might find himself associated with. It is certainly the case that two former team tennis players have, through serious injury, not only been unable to play in team matches but have also forfeited attendance at some of the social events associated with the 'tennis clique'.

With respect to the importance of clothing and equipment to the understanding of a sporting practice, in tennis one of the easiest distinctions is made with respect to the racket itself. For this 'new bourgeoisie' tennis is a recently discovered sport and evident in the newcomers' approach is an acute awareness of the distinctions associated with the equipment. On The Heath a tennis racket carries with it symbolic meaning. The old wooden Dunlop Maxply has been almost completely replaced by a variety of mid-heads and large heads in an exotic collection of materials ranging from magnesium alloy through fibreglass to carbon graphite. Such rackets carry not only a financial price tag but a symbolic one too. They allow for a categorisation of the newcomer, even prior to stepping on to the tennis court, allowing distinctions to be made between someone who doesn't really play tennis (the old and cheap or dug out of the cupboard wooden racket), the beginner (the metal or alloy Prince style large head) and the serious player (the carbon fibre graphite – indicating a financial investment of around £100 and therefore a likely measure of serious intent and ability in the sport itself).

The tennis courts themselves, in addition to providing the physical space in which the game is played, act as stages on which reputations may be won or lost. Their importance as a symbolic arena can be gauged by one incident involving a 'handicap' tournament for women. Feeling confident of the outcome, two first team players agreed with their 'non-team playing opponents' to play their match off a revised handicap in order to quicken the outcome of the game. This resulted in a slight increase of the handicap, and the non-team players duly won the match. The implications of defeat for the first team players were of such importance that after the game confusion reigned as to who had agreed to the revised handicap. Following frantic conversation with the tournament referee, also a first team player, the match was begun again and did not finish until 11.45 pm. By this time the first teamers had secured their expected victory, establishing not only a win but also what many saw as a 'correctness' in the result! Only those not immersed in the 'tennis playing practices' felt that the eventual winners had cheated.

The estate management, in order to facilitate court use and the maintenance of equipment such as tennis nets, measuring sticks, floodlights and backstop netting, leave the everyday control of facilities to what are identified as 'user groups'. As such a number of 'user group committees' have been created for tennis, squash, mother and toddler 'ladies circle', etc. Therefore effective control over how activities 'get done' resides in large measure with these

138

committees, especially when such committees comprise the most prolific users, which is certainly the case for tennis and squash. To the extent that the 'tennis committee' has created a set of practices as to how the game should be played, this has had the effect of helping limit participation to those who play the game in this way. Consequently, although on occasion one does see 'rabbits' on court (the condescending phrase of 'those who play properly' used to describe those who don't) it is rare to see them playing at the same time that 'serious' players are on the adjacent court. When this does happen it is likely that the 'rabbits' will terminate their game, with explanatory comments such as, 'We'd spoil their game with our mis-hit balls crossing their court all the time.' Dressed in casual clothing rather than the designer wear of the 'serious' player, such 'casual' players appear intimidated by the arrival of the 'serious' player.

The system used to 'obtain' a tennis court also possesses consequences, particularly for children's use of the facilities. One of the most often voiced criticisms of the children relates to their relatively limited use of the facilities: 'I don't understand why the kids don't play more, they have everything they need here, but instead they just hang around saying they're bored.' The children's attitude is not so surprising when one realises that in order to play a game of tennis or squash one needs to write one's name in an appropriate 'time slot' on the 'booking sheets' located in the recreational centre. During the most popular seasons for these sports, spring and summer for tennis, autumn and winter for squash, this usually means booking at least one week in advance in order to obtain the most popular, early evening playing times. However, for children and the casual player, tennis or squash is not the organised activity that it is for the 'serious' player. As such when children do appear on the courts at these times it is invariably because a court has suddenly become available. On certain occasions when this has happened 'serious' players have entered the recreational centre, crossed out the name of the person who had booked the court but failed to play and then returned to the court and dismissed the playing children for failing to comply with the rules for booking courts! When younger children do manage successfully to book courts at these times then the impatient 'serious' player will, on occasion, challenge those who they see as not playing the game 'properly'. Not wearing 'correct' clothes or footwear, not keeping score in the prescribed manner or

'Old-men' see journals on orient,

failing to change ends at the correct times are reasons that 'serious' players give for challenging children to 'either play properly or get off the court'.

An understanding of such behaviour would only be a partial understanding if it were to be simply seen as selfish. Attempts have been made by both 'serious' tennis and squash players to introduce children to their respective sports and for a very few children these have been successful in that they have taken up the sport in the manner deemed 'proper' by the 'serious' players. However, it is suggested that it is the control of the facility, and the practices that maintain that control, that underlie the distinctions that can be observed with respect to the frequency of the facilities' use. Conversations with occasional players, and with some of those who do not play at all, indicate the 'seriousness' with which the sports are played as one of the main obstacles that limit their involvement in the activity. The following comments are typical of those encountered in such conversations:

> 'the courts are always booked by the team players ... I'd like to occasionally but its difficult to get a court ... It might be fun but I'd feel such a fool, I can't play properly'.

CONCLUSION

We have attempted to describe the ways in which the recreational facilities are used and organised by residents of The Heath. The suggestion is that the two identified groups, 'drinkers' and 'sporters', can be understood to have their origins broadly within the social groups identified in the previous chapters, and that they engage in quite distinct leisure practices. Although 'drinkers' and 'sporters' share similar socio-economic backgrounds with respect to the father's occupation, both their educational experiences and current occupational positions can be differentiated. By employing Bourdieu's concept of habitus and his differentiation between economic and cultural capital, we have attempted to examine the distinctions in the leisure practices of these two fractions of the new middle class and have argued that such practices can be understood as one of the principal ways in which social position is constructed.

Both groups owe their existence to industrial and economic change in the post-war period and/or to the increase in higher education provision in the 1960s, although such provision has been relatively more important for the 'sporters'. In moving through the social space both groups have had to be geographically mobile but such geographical mobility is welcomed for the accompanying social mobility they see as having been attained. Indeed, as Bell (1968) comments, such geographical mobility is perhaps a necessary condition of social mobility.

Both groups, in Featherstone's (1987) terms, could be said to be the perfect consumers although their consumption patterns are very different. The 'drinkers' could be understood as constructing social position based very much on the promise of material success held out to working-class youth in the late 1950s and early 1960s, commented upon by Cohen (1972), albeit in different circumstances, in his analysis of Mod youth culture in the early 1960s. They are the working-class grammar school kids who 'made it'. Their sense of social position is constructed through a 'looking back' to their social origins. From where they are now – a detached house in the countryside, a company car and a suit for work – these and their leisure practices become part of a statement that affirms change. However, as an affirmation of change such practices, to be recognised in the parent culture, need to stay the same.

The 'sporters' engage in very different leisure practices, and construct social position through the promotion of a particular style of life related to the acquisition of cultural rather than economic capital. This group, largely college-educated, could be said to be searching more for the cultural requirements of middle class-ness such as those associated with an appreciation of culture used in this term's 'high or sacred sense'. As such their construction of social position concerns itself more with what is perceived as the 'correct' form of consumption than its amount. Their disposition towards certain leisure activities rather than others, and more so the practice of such dispositions, lends support to Bourdieu's contention that this class fraction can be seen to promote itself through the acquisition of cultural capital. Rather than a 'looking back', their's is a 'looking forward' – a search to acquire the cultural hallmarks that they associate with a class they see themselves as entering. As such their leisure practices, particularly their involvement with the 'learning mode', are essentially attempts at 'becoming'.

The struggle in the social space between these two fractions is evidenced by the way in which the leisure practices of each subverts the use of the facilities by others. The 'drinkers' have constructed the lounge bar in a way that best accommodates their use, while the 'sporters', through their creation of various competitions and rules associated with the use of the facilities, provide themselves with a series of opportunities to construct what they take to be a 'middle class-ness'. Both groups have succeeded in eliminating others from effective participation – effective in the sense that these activities are done on the terms of the group that controls the practices of use by which the facilities are used.

What this analysis points towards is the need for an examination of leisure practices, not as appendages to an existent lifestyle but as part of the construction and affirmation of social position. To observe that people drink and play tennis, or badminton, golf or rugby for that matter, is not enough. Neither is it enough simply to quantify the frequency with which these activities are done. A sociology of leisure must locate such leisure practices within a wider social order if it is to explain the nature of the choices made. The leisure practices outlined above are practices by which these class fractions announce and establish their positions, and they reflect the positions of these class fractions in the changing economy.

8

CONCLUSION

- Use in criticism of Bourdieu.
- Suggests that the classes are no longer defined as such.
- Postmodernity + individualism create desire for choosing leisure, ∴ lifestyles identified this way.

In this concluding chapter we will summarise the results of this case study and suggest possible directions for future research in the light of these results and in the context of current debate regarding the new middle class and contemporary cultural change. It has been argued that the sociological debate over the new middle class is one of the most pertinent to understanding the class restructuring currently taking place within British society. In addition we have argued that an examination of the changing cultural practices associated with this restructuring indicate that the new middle class cannot be understood as a single, unified collectivity but rather must be seen as *essentially* fragmented. However, rather than see such fragmentation as grounded in an existing hierarchy associated with an 'economism' which sees the occupational structure as the locus or orienting thematic from which cultural, taste and leisure preferences are understood, this study suggests that such cultural practices and tastes have an economy of their own, associated with occupational position but not determined by it. Indeed the analysis has suggested that a combination of variables, including social origin, education and gender, act to produce a 'structuring structure' – one dimension of the habitus – in accounting for what have been termed the social spaces of mobility, lifestyle and gender.

In the case study undertaken the majority of households on The Heath can be described as a recently affluent, socially and geographically mobile grouping. For some, educational qualifications are considerably higher than for the general population, yet at the same time many have not amassed extensive educational credentials. Even so the occupational positions and levels of income characterise the households as being materially successful.

143

Predominantly comprised of families with young children, the households enjoy a style of life associated with the possession of consumer durables of a consistently high material standard.

In reviewing the setting for this study it is clear that housing tenure is of the highest order. Virtually all of the residents are home-owners, with property in the highest priced categories. They are considerably more affluent than the majority of the population and this affluence is displayed in both the prices of their homes and the consumer goods that they enjoy. For many, conspicuous consumption is their hallmark, associated with 'consumer grazing' trips to the three cities that lie less than 30 miles from the estate, Chester, Liverpool and Manchester, as well as those 'southern' townships located in the Cheshire countryside, the 'home' county of the North. They are, in many cases, the 'working-class kids' of the 1950s and 1960s who have, in their own and their parents' words, 'made good' or 'done well for themselves'. They are also 'par excellence' members of what has come to be known as the new middle class.

For the majority of men occupations are primarily of a professional and/or managerial nature. For women in employment outside the home it is either of a professional nature, for those with the highest educational qualifications, or of an administrative or clerical type. As we have seen in our discussion of the structural characteristics of the sample, the new middle class, exemplified by The Heath's residents, can be seen to have developed from both the traditional middle and working classes, with almost 45 per cent of our sample having their social origins within the traditional working class. For this group educational qualifications alone provide only a partial explanation for their social mobility, obtained through entry into a variety of professions but most commonly through those associated with the public sector. A larger number of males from working-class backgrounds owe their membership of the new middle class to a mobility developed through a series of promotions in the workplace associated with a changing economy in which service industries and new technology have replaced traditional industrial activity, together with the emergence of a white-collar middle management. The growth of these new occupations in the latter half of the twentieth century, together with their management and administration, has provided opportunities for relatively high ranges of social mobility and such conditions have

144

created the 'social space' for the development of the new middle class. In this context it has been shown that social mobility from the working class has been achieved through both educational credentialism and promotions and other opportunities associated with an emergent service economy. In examining occupational backgrounds and the relationship between education, social origin and occupation the data indicated that while the majority of professionals are graduates, only one-third of managers have degrees. In relating this analysis to social origin, the finding that the highest levels of educational qualification are obtained by 30 per cent of those from working-class backgrounds and 40 per cent of those from middle-class backgrounds leads to the suggestion that any cultural cleavage within the new middle class may relate more to educational level and its corresponding effects upon occupational choice than to initial class of origin. The suggestion is that it is educational and other forms of capital, in combination with occupational activity, that differentiate within the new middle class. Further, they are associated with important cultural differences such that they give rise to 'a struggle in the social space' of the new middle classes which can be evidenced in other arenas of their everyday lives.

Our findings on provisioning and leisure in the domestic household have revealed little that was not already known from previous research. It is primarily women rather than their male partners who plan and manage the day-to-day work activities in the household and it is primarily women who accomplish these tasks. However, observable differences are apparent in the relationship between education and occupation. As far as domestic labour is concerned it is in those households with members educated to degree level and working in professional occupations, irrespective of social origin, that men and women are most likely to share domestic tasks. Similarly, in looking at the use of The Heath's clubhouse and sports facilities, our data suggests that the gendered differentials observed are modified with regard to the social origin, educational level and occupation of both the respondent and the household in which the respondent is located. In short, although differences between females are less apparent than those between males, they do nevertheless exist. Consequently, while we have been able to document significant differences in the leisure lifestyles of men and women it must be remembered that such differences impinge upon women quite

differently according to their social origins, educational qualifications and occupations. While the majority can be seen to operate
under similar constraints with regard to domestic labour, and
while differences in constraints and opportunities can also be
related to occupation, child care and the life cycle, nevertheless
important differences between women can be observed. Further,
such differences can be seen to relate to the principal concerns of
this study, namely the cultural fragmentation and heterogeneity
of the new middle classes.

In our examination of the use of the clubhouse and other leisure
and recreational activities it appears that it is those of working-
class origin who are the prime users of the clubhouse. The bar is
primarily associated with those who have the lowest educational
levels, and sports with those who have the highest educational
levels. The picture presented allows for the construction of what
has been termed the social space of lifestyles, suggesting that the
structuring characteristics of the habitus – social origin, education, gender, occupation and previous 'sporting' histories – act in
combination to produce differential responses in lifestyle choice.
Following Bourdieu, the analysis undertaken suggests that such
choices relate to everyday practices in which educational and
other capitals operate to differentiate amongst this new middle
class. It is in this way that we can see the habitus acting as a
structuring structure – making everyday practices the taken for
granted preferences – which results in the differentiations
observed in everyday life on The Heath, including the use made
and organisation of the clubhouse and other recreational facilities. Such a model indicates that the new middle classes exhibit a
series of lifestyle choices, structured by and structuring of their
respective habitus.

While these observations have been derived by employing a
conceptual schema associated with the work of Bourdieu (1984),
some of the results obtained question the convertibility of economic and cultural capital. As Savage et al. (1992:101–102) have
indicated, the relative importance of credentials in France for both
professionals and managerial 'cadres' makes the convertibility of
cultural into economic capital an important feature of the French
class structure. Indeed it could be argued that such convertibility
helps the French bourgeoisie to retain its homogeneity. In the
analysis undertaken here, and the emphasis placed on the cultural and economic restructuring of the middle class, it has been

146

Criticism of
Bourdieu's theories related in G.B !

argued that the new middle classes cannot be understood as a homogenous grouping precisely because of the different characteristics of those who occupy it. Given our findings pertaining to social origin, education and gender, it is not surprising that we should discover heterogeneity rather than homogeneity in the everyday social practices. Further, it is such heterogeneity, or fragmentation, that leads to the suggestion that traditional conceptions of class and the explanatory power of the class structure itself may be undergoing a fundamental change.

use to be critical

THE END OF CLASS? *of Bourdieu*

In Chapter 2 we identified a number of themes associated with the established debate on the structural position of the middle class in British society. In essence it was argued that class and the occupational structure were often confused and that a failing of many analyses was to assume that one could simply 'read' class structure from occupational position. Rather we suggested that occupations, together with factors such as their emergence, working conditions, gendered nature and professionalisation *were themselves* a part of class structuration. This theme was taken further when we criticised those theories of leisure that sought the explanation of contemporary leisure practices in a determinant relationship to type of occupation or class position. In succeeding chapters we related our findings of fragmentation to the view that in a society characterised by an emphasis on hedonism and consumption (Bourdieu, 1984:310) *leisure practices themselves become important locators of social identity.* Such views have become associated with a number of authors who have begun to examine the implications of postmodernist theorising for sociological investigation. In the argument developed below it is suggested that the findings from this study offer support to those positions that have sought to understand contemporary social change and the new middle class in the context of the emergence of a postmodern culture and an increasing individualisation of the social structure.

Postmodernist claims for 'the end of the social' may indeed have reflected a truth in the observation that 'the centre no longer holds', if, as sociologists, we locate that centre in 'relations to the means of production' (Baudrillard, 1981; Lyotard, 1984). Certainly, this study suggests that the interrelations between work, leisure, place and class are undergoing a transformation. However, of itself this is only a partial story. The divisions around consumption and the social construction of identity may be taking the place of those previously associated with work, and new social groups may be being formed around aesthetic and cultural divisions, located in experiences outside of work. While the subjects of this case study can be identified as members of a 'new middle class' in regard to their residence, occupation and income, it is their leisure practices that are amongst the most salient features of their everyday lives and that most clearly differentiate them from each other.

Related to these observations are those discussions that see the new middle class as 'new cultural intermediaries' (Featherstone, 1987 and 1991; Lash and Urry, 1987; Lash, 1990; Savage *et al.*, 1992). These arguments run contrary to those of 'conservatism' suggested by Goldthorpe (1987; 1995). Rather this work suggests that a particular class fraction of the new middle class acts as 'new cultural intermediaries' and can be seen to be involved in its own promotion, resulting from its emergence in the new 'service economy'. Featherstone's article, 'Lifestyle and consumer culture', (1987), begins with an analysis of Baudrillard and the claim of postmodernism to signal the 'end of meaning', a move towards a society beyond fixed status groups, producing a proliferation of signs which cannot be ultimately stabilised. However, rather than seeing such sign-consumption as producing the 'death of the social', Featherstone retrieves Baudrillard to suggest that

> the [post modernist] proclamation of a *beyond* [the social] is really a *within*, a new move within the intellectual game which takes into account the new circumstances of production of cultural goods, which will itself in turn be greeted as eminently marketable by the cultural intermediaries.
>
> (Featherstone, 1987:167)

This retrieval is accomplished by suggesting, à la Bourdieu, that social groups competing for control in particular social fields, use their relative amounts of economic and/or cultural capital accumulated to promote their own symbolic ordering in attempts to control such fields. For the new middle class it is argued that postmodernist cultural productions offer a schema whereby the new cultural producers together with other fractions of the middle class, the cultural intermediaries and 'service' professionals,

combine to promote their own cultural and economic productions in order to establish their position in a changing social
world,

> which judges people by their capacity for consumption,
> their 'standard of living', their lifestyle, as much as by their
> capacity for production.

(Bourdieu, 1984:310)

However, rather than a view of consumer culture as solely concerned with the purchase and display of consumer durables, its
impact has to be understood in all its forms. These include the
very making of culture itself, the legitimation practices that it
produces, together with its aesthetics. As such consumer culture
or commodity culture provides, like other cultural forms, the
means by which social structure is mediated to and by individuals. Consumer culture, like other cultures, provides the 'stuff'
that allows for such mediation. It is here that we would argue that
processes of cultural commodification have had a destabilising
effect on the very nature of the cultural and the individuals relationship to it, and that such a changed relationship casts some
doubt on the contemporary relevance of Bourdieu's original project in *Distinction*. In this context we have already suggested that
our observations regarding distinctions in social mobility paths
for the 'credentialed' and 'non-credentialed' create difficulties
with Bourdieu's model (Chapter 4). Our second point of depart-
ure relates to the very nature of contemporary cultural forms and
their promotion. Bourdieu's work is concerned with an *economy of
cultural practices* related to a hierarchical social order. However,
given the argument developed above, if a *new cultural economy* is
emerging, based on hedonism and enjoyment (Bourdieu,
1984:310), then to what extent may new cultural forms and productions challenge existing ones? To the extent that they do offer
such a challenge then we can speak of a new middle class not as
attempting to accquire the hallmarks of a traditional middle class,
à la Bourdieu, but rather modifying and replacing such hallmarks
through the promotion and creation of their own.

Further, to the extent that the changes referred to above have
penetrated the wider social structure, then Bourdieu's whole
schema is threatened. The society in which cultural propriety is
associated with an established cultural hierarchy engaged in a
particular set of cultural practices which it has made its own, is

challenged by new cultural practices associated with the commodification of cultural forms which threaten the very basis of
any established economy of cultural practices. Under these conditions such a threat is not solely a preserve of the new middle class,
but rather a more pervasive form of cultural change witnessed
throughout western societies and emergent throughout the latter
half of this century. If we consider this scenario, then what has
been described as 'the postmodern condition' (Lyotard, 1984) can
be understood as having penetrated contemporary society generally, rather than just a certain class fraction of the new middle
class. In this context, while postmodernism may have been taken
up by a class fraction of cultural intermediaries, we still need to
consider the conditions under which this class fraction has
emerged and the extent to which a postmodern culture may be
said to have become a cultural dominant.

We would argue that such changes have resulted in the
destabilisation of cultural hierarchies and taste distinctions such
that the social practice of distinction, and the resultant social edi-
fice it helps to reproduce, are themselves made problematic. As a
result, social identities may no longer be 'read' from class or
occupational position but rather exist as a combination of individual choices made available by these destabilising processes.

This 'individualisation' of the social has primarily been associated with the work of Ulrich Beck (1992:127–139). Beck argues
that contemporary society, characterised by 'reflexive modernity'
(Giddens, 1991), requires the individual to choose, precisely
because of the commodification processes referred to above. For
Beck, the very processes involved in the rationalising project of
modernity contain the seeds of an increasing individualisation of
the social. Through an examination of modernity's 'history' Beck
argues that the 'causes' of increasing individualisation – reflexive
modernity – can be seen in the following historical processes: first,
the gradual disappearance of the traditional working-class 'community'; second, the transferral of what were traditionally 'family
responsibilities' to the state and therefore the development of state
welfare; and, third, the destandardisation of labour or what, in
part, Lash and Urry (1987) have termed 'disorganised capitalism'.
Through such 'individualising' processes Beck argues that,

> The Individual himself or herself becomes the reproduction
> unit for the social in the life world ... People with the same

social, mobility

To understand the pertinence of this debate we need to examine the patterns of social mobility that have occurred in the latter half of this century, together with a recognition of the changing labour market and the social mobility experienced by significant numbers of what can be described as the traditional working class. As Goldthorpe (1987) has pointed out, such social mobility has been considerable, particularly so for the generation born during and at the end of World War II.

In addition, the new occupations created by technological change, the decline of primary manufacturing and the extractive industries, together with the increase in non-manual, service sector work, have seen the emergence of large numbers of white-collar workers. The geographical re-location of such work has also helped to bring about a decline in the strength of the relationship between class, occupation and residential location, and this too has contributed to the decline in traditional working-class communities. The associated emergence of developments such as The Heath, located in the 'new countryside' outside of both the city and traditional suburbia, has also ensured a weakening of the relationship between work, community and place.

These processes of individualisation have resulted in a reorientation of social and community life. No longer is it possible conveniently to 'read off' or locate leisure practices as integral and interrelated to work practices. Alongside the disappearance of traditional communities wedded to and formulated by work, by place and by social practice, we have, and are continuing to witness the emergence of, new 'places' like The Heath, where this trilateral relationship no longer exists. When work 'places' are often situated some 20 miles from 'home' and when the defining characteristics of occupations are no longer so easily identifiable in working practices, then, it is argued, alternative practices, outside and separate from work practices, will come to play an increasingly significant role in the construction of social identity.

This study has suggested that it is leisure practices, rather than work practices, that are most pertinent in understanding the social divisions that exist within this new middle class. While a homogeneity of sorts might still be presented through statistical correlations of occupation, income and residence, suggestive of a homogenous social grouping, close examination of leisure practices, together with a Bourdieuan analysis of cultural and economic capital, reveals significant differences which serve to fragment rather than solidify this new middle class. When these findings are allied to recent theoretical work on the cultural significance of the new middle class, and the suggestion that it is consumption rather than production through which social identities are increasingly formed, then many of the esoteric concerns of those living on The Heath – concerns relating to their dinner party invitations or their positions on the squash or tennis ladders – may, on reflection, appear less esoteric or obtuse than first thought.

APPENDIX

CODING

The following notes provide more details of the procedures used in the data analysis and will hopefully prove useful to those wishing a fuller understanding of how the quantitative work was undertaken.

The data was coded for analysis using SPSS and following an initial run of frequency distributions was analysed through a series of cross-tabulations which included variables such as parental occupation, occupation, income level and educational level. In this way it was possible to gain some measures of social origin, social mobility, educational capital, economic capital and occupational status. Following an analysis of these variables, and informed by both the ethnography and the interviews, the analysis that produced the diagrammatic models of the social spaces of mobility, lifestyle and gender was undertaken (Figures 4.1, 5.9 and 6.4). The diagrams are simply graphical representations of the relative positions of the social groups which make up The Heath. Taken together the diagrams show the 'homologies' associated with these differing social groups.

The occupational codings used were based on the Hope–Goldthorpe 'thirty-six point' scale of occupational ranking. The original table appears in Goldthorpe and Hope (1974:134–143). An extended discussion and review of the construction of the scale is contained in both Goldthorpe and Hope (1974) and Goldthorpe (1987). The scale was modified for ease of analysis into a five-point scale reflecting the frequency distributions obtained in the initial analysis. After an initial frequencies run the occupational variables were recoded into five categories as follows:

(1, 2, 10, 49 = 1) – professionals; (3, 4, 8, 14, 46 = 2) – senior–middle management private sector; (6, 11, 12, 13, 15 thru 35, 42, 45, 50 = 3) – technicians, skilled manual and supervisors); (5, 38 = 4) – unemployed and retired; (37, 70 = 5) – housewives (Table A.1).

Table A.1 Occupation recoded

Occupation recoded	Males (n = 217)	Females (n = 224)
Professionals	31.3	21.8
Management (private sector)	43.3	4.9
Technicians, supervisors and clerical	17.1	25.1
Unemployment and retired	8.3	3.6
Housewives	—	44.6

Parents' occupations were recoded as follows: (1 thru 3 = 1); (6, 8, 10, 11, 45, 49 = 2); (12 thru 16 = 3); (17 thru 35 = 4). (Table A.2).

Table A.2 Father's occupation recoded

Father's occupation recoded	Percentage (n = 217)
1 Professionals and senior managers	18.5
2 Administrative, middle managers and officials	22.6
3 Technicians, small proprietors and supervisors	15.2
4 Manual workers	43.7

Similar recodings were also undertaken for the education and income variables. Again these recodings reflect the statistical distributions obtained from an initial frequencies run. Educational qualifications were recoded into three categories as follows: (1 thru 3 = 1) (4 thru 6 = 2) (7, 8 = 3) 1 = low, 2 = medium, 3 = high (Tables A.3 and A.3 (a)).

Table A.3 Education

Education	Males (n = 214)	Females (n = 215)
1 None	6.5	14.4
2 School certificate	9.8	10.2
3 O levels	10.7	29.3
4 ONC	7.0	2.3
5 A levels	5.1	9.3
6 HNC	17.3	—
7 Degree	29.4	27.4
8 Higher degree/prof./qual	14.0	2.3

Table A.3 (a) Education recoded

Education recoded	Males (n = 214)	Females (n = 215)
1 Low	27.1	54.0
2 Medium	29.4	16.3
3 High	43.5	29.8

The income variable was recoded into three categories as follows: (1 = 1); (2, 3 = 2); (4, 5, 6 = 3): 1 = low, 2 = medium, 3 = high (Tables A.4 and A.4 (a)).

Table A.4 Income

Income	Males (n = 196)	Females (n = 130)
1 Under £10,000	10.7	76.9
2 £10 – 14,999	19.9	17.7
3 £15 – 19,999	30.1	0.8
4 £20 – 24,999	18.4	2.3
5 £25 – 29,999	8.2	1.5
6 Over £30,000	12.2	0.8

Table A.4 (a) Education recoded

Income recoded	Males (n = 196)	Females (n = 130)
1 Low	10.8	76.9
2 Medium	50.3	18.5
3 High	39.0	4.6

DATA TRANSFORMATIONS

Bourdieu: capital and habitus

To employ Bourdieu's concepts of the capitals and habitus, data transformations were made to combine the social origin and education variables of respondents to show how these relate in combination. This new variable was constructed by combining social origin (parent's occupation) with the educational level of respondents (Table A.5). Social origin was dichotomised into (1) 'working class' (supervisory manual and manual occupations)

Table A.5   Social origin/education (males)

Social origin/educational level	Percentage
w/c 'low' ed. (n = 48)	26
w/c 'high' ed. (n = 32)	19
m/c 'low' ed. (n = 53)	28
m/c 'high' ed. (n = 50)	27

and (2) 'middle class'. Education level was dichotomised into 'high' (degree level and higher) and 'low' (sub-degree level). The construction of this variable produces a fourfold classification associated with social origin and educational level: (1) 'working class/low education', (2) 'working class/high education', (3) 'middle class/low education, (4) 'middle class/high education'. In combining the variables in this way we are able to provide for two of the principal 'structuring' features of the habitus, while recognising, of course, that the concept of the habitus itself cannot be solely reduced to these variables.

SAMPLE

Given the relatively small number of households on the estate, its clear geographical boundaries and the known size of the population parameter, the questionnaire was administered and conducted through a census of households rather than a sample. The advantages of the sample in regard to time and labour costs through the reduction in the size of those investigated were unnecessary considerations given the size of the population parameter of 400 households. As Moser and Kalton indicate the required sample size for small populations of a few hundred may easily approach the population size given that the precision of sample results depends on the size of the sample itself, rather than the population covered.

> In such cases complete coverage is commonly aimed at, for it is not worth while to introduce the complexities of sampling in order to obtain the marginal savings created by leaving out a small number of the population units.
> (Moser and Kalton, 1970:55)

In this way problems relating to the statistical reliability of the results from sampling were overcome. As such the questionnaire data reported upon is clearly representative of the residents of The Heath apart from, of course, the relatively small number of residents who did not complete the questionnaire.

The questionnaire was delivered, by hand, to each of the 400 households on the estate and was collected between one and two weeks later. A total of 261 completed questionnaires were collected, indicating a response rate of 65%. At the same time it was ascertained that 14% of households were either unoccupied or that residents were in the process of an imminent house move, therefore having less interest in responding. As such a truer response rate could be estimated to be closer to 80 per cent of households living on The Heath.

BIBLIOGRAPHY

Abercrombie, N. and J. Urry 1983 *Capital, Labour and the Middle Classes*. London: Allen & Unwin.

Allen, J. and D. Massey (eds) 1988 *The Economy In Question*. London: Sage.

Anderson, B. 1983 *Imagined Communities*. London: Verso.

Bagguely, P. 1992 'Social change, the middle class and the emergence of "new social movements": a critical analysis', *Sociological Review* 40:26–48.

Bagguely, P., J. Mark-Lawson, D. Shapiro, J. Urry, S. Walby and A. Warde 1990 *Restructuring: Place, Class and Gender*. London: Sage.

Barlow, J. and M. Savage 1986 'Conflict and cleavage in a Tory heartland' *Capital and Class* 30:156–182.

Baudrillard, J. 1981 *For a Critique of the Political Economy of the Sign*. St. Louis, Mo.: Telos Press.

Bauman, Z. 1987 *Legislators and Interpreters: On Modernity, Post-modernity and the Intellectuals*. Cambridge: Cambridge University Press.

—— *Intimations of Postmodernity*. London: Routledge.

Beail, N. 1983 'Father involvement in pregnancy, birth, and early parenthood'. PhD Thesis, London University Institute of Education.

Beauregard, S. 1986 'The chaos and complexity of gentrification' in N. Smith and P. Williams (eds) *The Gentrification of the City*. London: Allen & Unwin.

Beck, U. 1992 *Risk Society: Towards a New Modernity*. London: Sage.

Bell, C. 1968 *Middle Class Families: Social and Geographical Mobility*. London: Routledge & Kegan Paul.

Bell, C. and S. Encel (eds) 1978 *Inside the Whale: Ten Personal Accounts of Social Research*. Oxford: Pergamon Press.

Bell, C. and H. Newby 1971 *Community Studies*. London: George Allen and Unwin.

Bell, D. 1974 *The Coming of Post Industrial Society*. New York: Basic Books.

—— 1976 *The Cultural Contradictions of Capitalism*. London: Heinemann.

Berger, B. 1969 *Working Class Suburb*. London: Cambridge University Press.

Berger, P. 1966 *Invitation to Sociology*. Harmondsworth: Pengiun Books.

Berger, P., B. Berger and H. Kellner 1974 *The Homeless Mind*. Harmondsworth: Pelican Books.
Berger, P. and T. Luckmann 1971 *The Social Construction of Reality*. Harmondsworth: Penguin Books.
Berking, H. and S. Neckel 1993 'Urban marathon: the staging of individuality as an urban event' *Theory, Culture and Society* 10 (4):63–78.
Berman, M. 1983 *All that is solid melts into air*. London: Verso.
—— 1992 'Why modernism still matters' in S. Lash and J. Friedman (eds.) *Modernity and Identity*. Oxford: Blackwell.
Best, F. 1976 *The Future of Work*. Englewood Cliffs, NJ: Prentice-Hall.
Betz, H. 1992 'Postmodernism and the new middle class' *Theory, Culture and Society* 9 (2):93–114.
Bianchini, F. and M. Parkinson (eds) 1994 *Cultural Policy and Urban Regeneration*. Manchester: Manchester University Press.
Bianchini, F. and H. Schwengel 1991 'Re-imagining the city' in J. Corner and S. Harvey (eds) *Enterprise and Heritage*. London: Routledge.
Bonner, F. and P. Du Gay 1992a 'Representing the enterprising self: *thirtysomething* and contemporary consumer culture' *Theory, Culture and Society* 9 (2):67–92.
—— 1992b '*Thirtysomething* and contemporary consumer culture: distinctiveness and distinction' in R. Burrows and C. Marsh (eds) *Consumption and Class*. London: Macmillan.
Bottomore, T. 1965 *Classes in Modern Society*. London: George Allen and Unwin.
Bourdieu, P. 1966 *Elites in Society*. Harmondsworth: Penguin.
—— 1977 *Outline of a Theory of Practice*. Cambridge: Cambridge University Press.
—— 1984 *Distinction: A Social Critique of the Judgement of Taste*. London: Routledge & Kegan Paul.
—— 1985 'The social space and the genesis of groups' *Theory and Society* 14:723–744.
Bourdieu, P. and J. Passeron 1977 *Reproduction In Education, Society and Culture*. London: Sage.
Bracey, H. 1964 *Neighbours: On New Estates and Subdivisions in England and U.S.A.* London: Routledge & Kegan Paul.
Bramham, P. and I. Henry (eds) 1989 *Leisure and Urban Processes: Critical Studies of Leisure Policy in Western European Cities*. London: Routledge.
Bramham, P. and J. Spink 1994 'Leisure and the postmodern city' in I. Henry (ed.) *Leisure: Modernity, Postmodernity and Lifestyles*. The Leisure Studies Association, Chelsea School Research Centre, University of Brighton.
Brannen, J. and P. Moss 1991 *Managing Mothers: Dual Earner Households after Maternity Leave*. London: Unwin Hyman.
Braverman, H. 1974 *Labour and Monopoly Capital: the Degradation of Work in the Twentieth Century*. New York: Monthly Review Press.
Breen, R. and D. Rottman 1995 'Class analysis and class theory', *Sociology* 29 (3):453–473.
Brubaker, R. 1985 'Rethinking classical theory', *Theory and Society* 14:745–775.

Bryson, L. and F. Thompson 1978 'Reflections on an Australian newtown' in Bell C. and S. Encel (eds) *Inside the Whale: Ten Personal Accounts of Social Research*. Oxford: Pergamon Press.

Burris, V. 1986 'The discovery of the new middle class', *Theory and Society* 15:317–349.

Burrows, R. and C. Marsh (eds) 1992a *Consumption and Class*. London: Macmillan.

—— 1992b 'Consumption, class and contemporary sociology' in R. Burrows and C. Marsh (eds) *Consumption and Class*. London: Macmillan.

Butler, T. and M. Savage (eds) 1995 *Social Change and the Middle Classes*. London: UCL Press.

Calhoun, C., E. Lipuma and M. Postone 1993 *Bourdieu: Critical Perspectives*. Chicago: University of Chicago Press.

Chambers, I. 1990 *Border Dialogues*. London: Routledge.

Clarke, J and C. Critcher 1985 *The Devil Makes Work*. London: Macmillan.

Clarke, J., C. Modgil and S. Modgil (eds) 1990 *John H. Goldthorpe: Consensus and Controversy*. London: Falmer.

Cohen, P. 1972 'Subcultural conflict and working class community'. Working Papers in Cultural Studies, 2. Centre for Contemporary Cultural Studies, University of Birmingham.

Cooke, P. 1988 'Modernity, postmodernity and the city', *Theory, Culture and Society* 5(2–3).

Corrigan, P. and D. Sayer 1985 *The Great Arch*. Oxford: Blackwell.

Crane, D. 1992 *The Production of Culture*. London: Sage.

Crompton, R. 1989 'Class theory and gender' *British Journal of Sociology* 40 (4): 565–587.

—— 1990 'Goldthorpe and Marxist theories of historical development' in J. Clarke, C. Modgil and S. Modgil (eds) *John H. Goldthorpe: Consensus and Controversy*. London: Falmer.

—— 1992 'Patterns of social consciousness amongst the middle classes' in R. Burrows and C. Marsh (eds) *Consumption and Class*. Basingstoke: Macmillan.

—— 1993 *Class and Stratification: An Introduction to Current Debates*. Cambridge: Polity Press.

—— 1995 'Women's employment and the "middle class"' in T. Butler and M. Savage (eds) *Social Change and the Middle Classes*. London: UCL Press.

Crompton, R. and M. Mann (eds) 1994 *Gender and Stratification*. 2nd edn. Cambridge: Polity Press.

Dawe, A. 1970 'The two sociologies' *British Journal of Sociology* 21:207–218.

De Certeau, M. 1984 *The Practice of Everyday Life*. Berkeley: University of California Press.

De Grazia, S. 1962 *Of Time, Work and Leisure*. New York: Twentieth Century Fund.

Deem, R. 1986 *All Work and No Play?* Milton Keynes: Open University Press.

Dempsey, K. 1988 'Men's leisure, women's leisure: an Australian case study of appropriation and exclusion'. Paper presented at Leisure Studies Association 2nd International Conference: June/July. University of Sussex.

Dennis, N., F. Henriques and C. Slaughter 1969 *Coal Is Our Life*. London: Tavistock.

Devine, F. 1992a 'Social identity, class identity and political perspectives' *Sociological Review* 40:229–252.

—— 1992b *Affluent Workers Revisited: Privatism and the Working Class*. Edinburgh: Edinburgh University Press.

Dickens, P. 1988 *One Nation? Social Change and the Politics of Locality*. London: Pluto.

Dumazadier, J. 1974 *Sociology of Leisure*. Amsterdam: Elsevier.

Durkheim, E. 1964 *The Division of Labour in Society*. New York: Free Press.

Edgell, S. 1980 *Middle Class Couples*. London: George Allen and Unwin.

—— 1993 *Class*. London: Routledge.

Edgell, S. and V. Duke 1991 *A Measure of Thatcherism: A Sociology of Britain*. London: HarperCollins.

Ehrenreich, B. 1989 *Fear of Falling: The Inner Life of the Middle Class*. New York: Pantheon Books.

Elliot, B., D. McCrone and F. Bechhofer 1988 'Anxieties and ambitions: the *petit bourgeoisie* and the New Right in Britain' in D. Rose (ed.) *Social Stratification and Economic Change*. London: Hutchinson.

Emmison, M. and M. Western 1990 'Social class and social identity: a comment on Marshall *et al.*, *Sociology* 24:241–253.

Entwistle, D. R. and S. G. Doering 1980 *The First Birth*. Baltimore: Johns Hopkins University Press.

Epstein, A. L. (ed.) 1967 *The Craft of Social Anthropology*. London: Tavistock Publications.

Featherstone, M. 1987 'Lifestyle and consumer culture'. In E. Meijer (ed.) *Everyday Life: Leisure and Culture*. Department of Leisure Studies, University of Tilburg, The Netherlands.

—— 1991 *Consumer Culture and Postmodernism*. London: Sage.

Fielding, A.J. and M. Savage 1987 'Social mobility and the changing class composition of south east England'. University of Sussex Working Paper in Urban and Regional Studies, No. 60.

Gans, H. J. 1962 *The Urban Villagers*. New York: Free Press.

Giddens, A. 1980 *The Class Structure of the Advanced Societies*. 2nd edn. London: Hutchinson.

—— 1984 *The Constitution of Society*. Cambridge: Polity Press.

—— 1987 *Social Theory and Modern Sociology*. Cambridge: Polity Press.

—— 1990 *The Consequences of Modernity*. Oxford: Polity.

—— 1991 *Modernity and Self Identity: Self and Society in the Late Modern Age*. Oxford: Polity.

Giddens, A. and D. Held (eds) 1982 *Classes, Power, and Conflict*. London: Macmillan.

Giddens, A. and G. Mackenzie (eds) 1982 *Social Class and the Division of Labour*. Cambridge: Cambridge University Press.

BIBLIOGRAPHY

Gilroy, P. 1987 *Ain't No Black in the Union Jack*. London: Routledge.

Glyptis, S., H. McInnes and A. Patmore 1987 *Leisure and the Home*. London: Sports Council/ESRC.

Goffman, E. 1969 *The Presentation of Self in Everyday Life*. London: Allen Lane.

Goldthorpe, J. H. 1982 'On the service class, its formation and future' in A. Giddens and G. MacKenzie (eds) *Social Class and the Division of Labour*. Cambridge: Cambridge University Press.

—— 1983 'Women and class analysis: in defence of the conventional view' *Sociology* 17:465–488.

—— 1984 'Women and class analysis: a reply to the replies' *Sociology* 18:491–499

—— 1987 *Social Mobility and Class Structure In Modern Britain*. 2nd edn. Oxford: Clarendon Press.

—— 1988 'Intellectuals and the working class in modern Britain' in D. Rose (ed.) *Social Stratification and Economic Change*. London: Hutchinson.

—— 1995 'The service class revisited' in T. Butler and M. Savage (eds) *Social Change and the Middle Classes*. London: UCL Press.

Goldthorpe, J. H. and K. Hope 1974 *The Social Grading of Occupations*. Oxford: Clarendon Press.

Goldthorpe, J. H., D. Lockwood, F. Bechhofer and J. Platt 1969 *The Affluent Worker in the Class Structure*. Cambridge: Cambridge University Press.

Goldthorpe, J. H. and G. Marshall 1992 'The promising future of class analysis: a response to recent critiques' *Sociology* 26:381–400.

Goode, W. J. 1970 *World Revolution and Family Patterns*. London: Collier-Macmillan.

Gorz, A. 1982 *Farewell To The Working Class*. London: Pluto.

Graham, H. and L. Mckee 1979 'The first months of motherhood'. Report on a Health Education Council Project concerned with women's experience of pregnancy, childbirth and the first six months after birth. Mimeograph, University of York.

Gramsci, A. 1971 *Selections from the Prison Notebooks*. London: Lawrence and Wishart.

Green, E., S. Hebron and D. Woodward 1987 'Women's leisure, constraints and opportunities'. Leisure Studies Association paper. Eastbourne: Leisure Studies Association.

—— 1990 *Women's Leisure, What Leisure?* Basingstoke: Macmillan Education.

Gregory, D. and J. Urry (eds) 1985 *Social Relations and Spatial Structures*. London: Macmillan.

Griffen, C. 1985 *Typical Girls?* London: Routledge.

Hakim, C. 1987 *Research Design*. London: Routledge.

Hall, J. 1990 'Bourdieu, cultural capital, and cultural theories of stratification: a revisionist critique', Mimeograph, Department of Sociology, University of California, Davis, CA.

Hall, S. and M. Jacques (eds) 1989 *New Times*. London: Lawrence and Wishart.

Hall, S. and T. Jefferson (eds) 1976 *Resistance Through Rituals*. London: Hutchinson.

Hammond, J. and P. Williams 1986 'Yuppies' *Public Opinion Quarterly* 50:487–501.

Hamnett, C., L. McDowell and P. Sarre 1989 *The Changing Social Structure*. London: Sage.

Hargreaves, J. 1986 *Sport, Power and Culture*. Cambridge: Polity.

Harvey, D. 1989 *The Condition of Postmodernity*. Oxford: Blackwell.

Hatt, P. K. and A. J. Reiss, Jr. (eds) 1963 *Cities and Society*. New York: Free Press.

Hebdige, D. 1979 *Subculture*. London: Methuen.

—— 1987 *Cut 'n' Mix*. London: Comedia.

—— 1988 *Hiding In The Light*. London: Comedia.

Henry, I. 1993 *The Politics of Leisure Policy*. London: Macmillan.

—— (ed.) 1994 *Leisure: Modernity, Postmodernity and Lifestyles*. The Leisure Studies Association, Chelsea School Research Centre, University of Brighton.

Hewison, R. 1987 *The Heritage Industry*. London: Methuen.

Hochschild, A. 1989 *The Second Shift: Working Parents and the Revolution at Home*. New York: Viking Penguin.

Hoggart, R. 1958 *The Uses of Literacy*. Harmondsworth: Pelican Books.

Holton, R. and B. Turner 1994 'Debate and pseudo-debate in class analysis: some unpromising aspects of Goldthorpe and Marshall's defence' *Sociology* 28 (3):799–804.

Hunt, P. 1980 *Gender and Class Consciousness*. London: Macmillan.

Jager, M. 1986 'Victoriana in Melbourne' in N. Smith and P. Williams (eds) *The Gentrification of the City*. London: Allen & Unwin.

Jenkins, R. 1983 *Lads, Citizens And Ordinary Kids*. London: Routledge & Kegan Paul.

—— 1992 *Pierre Bourdieu*. London: Routledge.

Jones, S. 1986 *Workers At Play*. London: Routledge & Kegan Paul.

Kaplan, M. 1975 *Leisure: Theory and Practice*. New York: Wiley.

Keat, R. and J. Urry 1982 *Social Theory as Science*. 2nd edn. London: Routledge & Kegan Paul.

Kellner, D. 1992 'Popular culture and the construction of postmodern identities' in S. Lash and J. Friedman (eds) *Modernity and Identity*. Oxford: Blackwell.

Kellner, H. and F. Heuberger (eds) 1991 *Hidden Technocrats: The New Class and the New Capitalism*. New York: Transaction Press.

Kelly, J. 1983 *Leisure Identities and Interactions*. London: George Allen and Unwin.

Kerr, M. 1958 *The People of Ship Street*. London: Routledge & Kegan Paul.

Kriesi, H. 1989 'New social movements and the new class in the Netherlands' *American Journal of Sociology* 94:1078–1116.

Lamont, M. 1990 'The Refined, the virtuous, and the prosperous: exploring symbolic boundaries in the French and American upper-middle class'. Paper presented at the 85th meeting of the American Sociological Association, Washington D.C.

—— 1992 *Money, Morals and Manners: The Culture of the French and of the Upper American Middle Class*. Chicago: University of Chicago Press.

Lash, S. 1990 *Sociology of Postmodernism*. London: Routledge.

Lash, S. and J. Urry 1987 *The End of Organised Capitalism*. Cambridge: Polity.

Lash, S. and J. Urry 1994 *Economies of Signs and Spaces*. London: Sage.

Lee, D. J. 1994 'Class as a social fact' *Sociology* 24:397–415.

Lyotard, J.F. 1984 *The Postmodern Condition*. Manchester: Manchester University Press.

McNall, S. G., R. F. Levine and R. Fantasia 1991 *Bringing Class Back In*. New York: Westview Press.

Marshall, G., H. Newby, D. Rose and C. Vogler 1988 *Social Class in Modern Britain*. London: Hutchinson.

Martin, B. 1981 *A Sociology of Contemporary Cultural Change*. Oxford: Blackwell.

—— 1991 'Qualitative market research in Britain: a profession on the frontiers of postmodernity' in H. Kellner and F. Heuberger (eds) *Hidden Technocrats: The New Class and the New Capitalism*. New York: Transaction Press.

Meijer, E. (ed.) 1987 *Everyday Life: Leisure and Culture*. Department of Leisure Studies, University of Tilburg, The Netherlands.

Miller, S. M. 1960 'Comparative social mobility' *Current Sociology* IX (1):1–89.

Mitchell, J. C. 1967 'On quantification in social anthropology' in A. L. Epstein (ed.) *The Craft of Social Anthropology*. London: Tavistock Publications.

Moorhouse, H. 1989 'Models of work, models of leisure' in C. Rojek *Leisure for Leisure*. London: Macmillan.

Mort, F. 1989 'The politics of consumption' in S. Hall and M. Jacques (eds) *New Times*. London: Lawrence and Wishart.

Moser, C. A. and G. Kalton 1971 *Survey Methods in Social Investigation*. London: Heinemann Educational Books.

Moss, P., G. Bolland and R. Foxman 1987 'The division of household work during the transition to parenthood' *Journal of Reproductive and Infant Psychology* 5.

Murphy, R. 1986 'Weberian closure theory: a contribution to the ongoing assessment', *The British Journal of Sociology* 37:21–41.

Newby, H. 1979 *Green and Pleasant Land*. Harmondsworth: Penguin.

Newson, J. and E. Newson 1963 *Infant Care in the Urban Community*. London: George Allen and Unwin.

Oakley, A. 1974 *The Sociology of Housework*. Oxford: Martin Robertson.

O'Connor, J. And D. Wynne 1991 'The uses and abuses of popular culture' *Loisier et Societe* 14 (2):465–482.

—— 1993 'From the margins to the centre'. Working Papers in Popular Cultural Studies No. 7. Manchester Institute for Popular Culture, Manchester Metropolitan University.

—— 1996 'Left loafing' in J. O'Connor and D. Wynne (eds) *From the Margins to the Centre*. Aldershot: Arena.

Pahl, J. M. and R. Pahl 1971 *Managers and Their Wives*. London: Allen Lane.

Pahl, R. 1984 *Divisions of Labour*. Oxford: Basil Blackwell.

Pahl, R. and C. D. Wallace 1988 'Neither angels in marble nor rebels in red: privatization and working-class consciousness' in D. Rose (ed.) *Social Stratification and Economic Change*. London: Hutchinson.

Park, R. E. 1952 *Human Communities: The City and Human Ecology*. New York: Free Press.

Parker, S. 1971 *The Future of Work and Leisure*. London: MacGibbon & Kee.

—— 1983 *Leisure and Work*. London: George Allen and Unwin.

Parkin, F. 1979 *The Marxist Theory of Class: A Bourgeois Critique*. London: Tavistock.

Parsons, T. 1952 *The Social System*. London: Routledge & Kegan Paul.

Payne, G. 1987 *Mobility and Change in Modern Society*. London: Methuen.

—— 1992 'Competing views of contemporary social mobility and social divisions' in R. Burrows and C. Marsh (eds) *Consumption and Class*. London: Macmillan.

Przeworski, A. 1985 *Capitalism and Social Democracy*. Cambridge: Cambridge University Press.

Relph, E. 1976 *Place and Placelessness*. London: Pion.

Richards, M. P., J. F. Dunn and B. Antonis 1977 'Caretaking in the first year of life', *Child: Care, Health and Development* 3 (1):23–36.

Roberts, K. 1978 *Contemporary Society and the Growth of Leisure*. London: Longman.

—— 1980 *Leisure*. 2nd edn. London: Longman.

Roberts, K., J. Cooke, A. Clarke and E. Semeonoff 1977 *The Fragmentary Class Structure*. London: Heinemann.

Rojek, C. 1985 *Capitalism and Leisure Theory*. London: Tavistock.

—— 1994 'Leisure and the dreamworld of modernity' in I. Henry (ed.) *Leisure: Modernity, Postmodernity and Lifestyles*. The Leisure Studies Association, Chelsea School Research Centre, University of Brighton.

—— 1995 *Decentring Leisure*. London: Sage.

Rose, D. 1984 'Rethinking gentrification: beyond the uneven development of Marxist urban theory', *Environment and Planning D: Society and Space* 1:47–74.

—— (ed.) 1988 *Social Stratification and Economic Change*. London: Hutchinson.

Rupp, J. 1992 'How mass is popular culture? Inconsistencies in Pierre Bourdieu's cultural capital theory', Mimeograph. The Amsterdam School For Social Research, University of Amsterdam, The Netherlands.

Russell, G. 1983 *The Changing Role of Fathers*. St. Lucia, Queensland: University of Queensland Press.

Saunders, P. 1986 *Social Theory and the Urban Question*. 2nd edn. London: Hutchinson.

—— 1990 *Social Class and Stratification*. London: Tavistock.

Savage, M. 1987 'Spatial mobility and the professional labour market', University of Sussex Working Paper in Urban and Regional Studies. No. 56.

—— 1988 'The missing link? The relationship between spatial mobility and social mobility' *British Journal of Sociology* 39(4).

Savage, M., P. Dickens and A. J. Fielding 1988 'Some social and political implications of the contemporary fragmentation of the service class' *International Journal of Urban and Regional Research* 12.

Savage, M., J. Barlow, P. Dickens and T. Fielding 1992 *Property, Bureaucracy and Culture: Middle Class Formation in Contemporary Britain.* London: Routledge.

Savage, M., P. Watt and S. Arber 1991 'Social class, consumption divisions and housing mobility' in R. Burrows and C. Marsh (eds) *Consumption and Class.* London: Macmillan.

Schulze, G. 1993 *Die Erlebnisgesellschaft: Kultursoziologie der Gegenwart.* Frankfurt: Campus Verlag.

Scott, J. 1994 'Class analysis: back to the future' *Sociology* 28:933–942.

Seeley, J. R., R. A. Sim and E. W. Loosley 1963 *Crestwood Heights.* New York: Wiley.

Sharpe, S. 1984 *Double Identity: The Lives of Working Mothers.* Harmondsworth: Penguin.

Shields, R. 1991 *Places on the Margin.* London: Routledge.

—— 1992a 'A truant proximity: presence and absence in the space of modernity' *Environment and Planning D: Society and Space* 10:181–198.

—— (ed.) 1992b *Lifestyle Shopping.* London: Routledge.

Simmel, G. 1963 'The metropolis and mental life' in P. K. Hatt and A. J. Reiss, Jr. (eds) *Cities and Society.* New York: Free Press.

Slater, E. and M. Woodside 1951 *Patterns of Marriage.* London: Cassell.

Smart, B. 1993 *Postmodernity.* London: Routledge.

Smith, N. 1987 'Of yuppies and housing: gentrification, social restructuring and the urban dream' *Environment and Planning D: Society and Space* 5:151–172.

Smith, N. and P. Williams (eds) 1986 *The Gentrification of the City.* London: Allen & Unwin.

Stedman-Jones, G. 1983 *Languages of Class.* Cambridge: Cambridge University Press.

Sulkunen, P. 1992 *The European New Middle Class.* Aldershot: Avebury.

Sulkunen, P., J. Holmwood, H. Radner and G. Schulze 1997 *Constructing the New Consumer Society.* London: Macmillan.

Thompson, E. P. 1963 *The Making of the English Working Class.* London: Gollancz.

Thrift, N. 1987 'The geography of late twentieth century class formation' in N. Thrift and P. Williams (eds) *Class and Space.* London: Routledge.

—— 1989 'Images of social change' in C. Hamnett, L. McDowell and P. Sarre (eds) *The Changing Social Structure.* London: Sage.

—— 1993 'An urban impasse?' *Theory, Culture and Society* 10 (2):229–237.

Thrift, N. and P. Williams 1987 *Class and Space.* London: Routledge.

Toffler, A. 1970 *Future Shock.* New York: Random House.

Tomlinson, A. (ed.) 1990 *Consumption, Identity and Style: Marketing, Meanings and the Packaging of Pleasure.* London: Routledge.

Touraine, A. 1971 *The Post-Industrial Society.* New York: Random House.

Turner, V. 1969 *The Ritual Process: Structure and Anti-Structure.* London: Allen Lane.

Urry, J. 1981 *The Anatomy of Class Societies: The Economy, Civil Society and the State*. London: Macmillan.
—— 1985 'Social relations, space and time' in D. Gregory and J. Urry (eds) *Social Relations and Spatial Structures*. London: Macmillan.
van der Poel, H. 1994 'The modularisation of daily life' in I. Henry (ed.) *Leisure: Modernity, Postmodernity and Lifestyles*. The Leisure Studies Association, Chelsea School Research Centre, University of Brighton.
Veblen, T. [1925] 1970 *The Theory of The Leisure Class*. London: Allen & Unwin.
Vidich, A. J. and J. Bensman 1968 *Small Town in Mass Society: Class, Power and Religion in a Rural Community*. Revised edn. Princeton: Princeton University Press.
Wacquant, L. 1988 'From ideology to symbolic violence: class, culture and consciousness in Marx and Bourdieu'. Mimeograph, Department of Sociology, The University of Chicago, Chicago.
—— 1991 'Making class: the middle class(es) in social theory and social structure' in S. G. McNall, R. F. Levine and R. Fantasia (eds) *Bringing Class Back In*. New York: Westview Press.
Walvin. J. 1978 *Leisure and Society 1830–1950*. London: Longman.
Warde, A. 1992 'Notes on the relationship between production and consumption' in R. Burrows and C. Marsh (eds) *Consumption and Class*. London: Macmillan.
—— 1994 'Consumption, identity-formation and uncertainty' *Sociology* 28:877–898.
Watson, W.1964 'Social mobility and social class in industrial communities' in M. Gluckman and E. Devons (eds) *Closed Systems and Open Minds*. Edinburgh: Oliver and Boyd.
Weber, M. 1949 *The Methodology of the Social Sciences*. New York: Free Press.
—— 1964 *The Theory of Social and Economic Organization*. New York: Free Press.
Whimster, S. 1992 'Yuppies: a keyword of the 1980s' in L. Budd and S. Whimster (eds) *Global Finance and Urban Living*. London: Sage.
Whyte, W. F. 1943 *Street Corner Society*. Chicago: University of Chicago Press.
Whyte, W. H. 1956 *The Organization Man*. New York: Simon and Schuster.
Wild, R. 1978 'The background to Bradstow' in C. Bell and S. Encel (eds) *Inside the Whale: Ten Personal Accounts of Social Research*. Oxford: Pergamon Press.
Williams, W. M. 1956 *The Sociology of an English Village: Gosforth*. London: Routledge.
Wirth, L. 1963 'Urbanism as a way of life' in P. K. Hatt and A. J. Reiss, Jr. (eds) *Cities and Society*. New York: Free Press.
Wynne, D. 1990 'Leisure, lifestyle and the construction of social position', *Leisure Studies* 9: 21–34.
—— (ed.) 1992 *The Culture Industry*. Aldershot: Avebury.
Wynne, D. and J. O'Connor 1992 'Tourists, hamburgers and street musicians' in R. Reichardt and G. Muskens (eds) *Post-communism, the*

Market and the Arts: First Sociological Assessments. Frankfurt am Main: Verlag Peter Lang.

Wynne, D., J. O'Connor and D. Phillips 1995 'City cultures and the new cultural intermediaries'. BSA Annual Conference, Leicester University. Forthcoming 1996 in *Opiniao Publica* IV (1).

Young, M. and P. Willmott 1960 *Family and Class in a London Suburb.* London: Routledge.

Zukin, S. 1987 'Gentrification: culture and capital in the urban core' *Annual Review of Sociology* 13:129–147.

—— 1988 *Loft Living: Culture and Capital in Urban Change.* London: Radius.

—— 1988b 'The postmodern debate over urban form' *Theory, Culture and Society* 5(2–3).

—— 1992a 'Postmodern urban landscapes: mapping culture and power' in S. Lash and J. Freidman (eds) *Modernity and Identity.* Oxford: Blackwell.

—— (1992), *Landscapes of Power: From Detroit to Disneyworld.* Berkeley: University of California Press.

Zweig, F. 1961 *The Worker in an Affluent Society.* London: Heinemann.

INDEX